Going Through Puberty

A girl's Manual for Body, Mind & Health

Going Through Puberty

A *girl's* Manual for Body, Mind & Health

Ruth J. Hickman, MD

Lesson Ladder
Success within reach!

www.lessonladder.com
21 Orient Street, Melrose, MA 02176

Lesson Ladder/XAMonline, Inc., Melrose, MA 02176

Lesson Ladder: An Imprint of XAMonline, Inc.
21 Orient Street
Melrose, MA 02176
Toll Free 1-800-301-4647
Web: www.lessonladder.com

Illustrations: Beehive Illustration
Cover, interior design, and composition:
Delgado and Company, Inc.
Acquisitions editor: Beth Kaufman
Project management and production supervision:
Elizabeth A. St. Germain

Library of Congress Catalog Card Number:
(pending)

Hickman, Ruth. .
Going through puberty: A girl's manual for body, mind
and health. / Ruth Hickman.
144 pp., 54 ill.

1. Title 2. Puberty 3. Puberty—psychology. 4. Parent and
teenager 5. Teenage girls

HQ797 H53 2013   612.661 H6286 2013

ISBN: 978-098-844-9909

This book is intended to educate and provide general
information about puberty and child development.
This book should not, however, be construed to
dispense medical services or be used to diagnose or
treat any medical condition. All questions and decisions about medical care should be addressed directly
with qualified health-care professional, including your
child's pediatrician. Accordingly, you are encouraged
to consult your personal health-care provider before
adopting any of the suggestions in this book or
drawing inferences from it.

While the author, editor and publisher have
endeavored to prepare an accurate and helpful book,
they make no representations or warranties, express or
implied,with respect to the accuracy or completeness
of its contents and specifically disclaim any warranties
of merchantability or fitness for a particular purpose.
The author, editor and publisher do not assume and
hereby disclaim any liability to any party for any loss,
damage or injury caused, directly or indirectly, by any
error, omission or information provided in this book.

The names, conditions and identifying details of
people associated with the events and advice
described in this book have been changed to protect
their privacy. Any similarities to actual individuals are
merely coincidental.

Published 2013

Printed in the United States

1 2 3 4 5 6 7 13 12 11 10 09 08

For all of today's girls and boys who will soon become the young women and men of tomorrow. Here's to your healthy growth and development in all arenas!

Dr. H

Acknowledgments

The author would like to thank the following individuals who worked tirelessly to make these books a reality: my husband, Will Hickman, for reviewing early drafts of this book; Sharon Wynne, President and CEO of Lesson Ladder; Elizabeth Heller, Professional Writer; Kassi Radomski, Developmental Editor; Beth Kaufman, Parenting Editor; Lisa Delgado, Interior and Cover Designer, Elizabeth St. Germain, Production Supervisor and Project Manager; the talented artists of Beehive Illustration—Gemma Hastilow, Moreno Chiacchiera; Bo Sherman, Director of Sales for Lesson Ladder; Dianne Liu, Marketing Manager for Lesson Ladder; Anna Wong, Assistant Editor; Nancy Brown, Editorial Assistant.

Above all, we would like to thank all the girls, boys, and parents who gave permission to be interviewed and provided multiple insights and quotes within these pages.

About the Author

Ruth Jessen Hickman, MD, has long been fascinated by questions of health, medicine, and life science. She is very proud of this book, in which she shares her knowledge with young adolescents.

Originally from Eastern Kentucky, Dr. Hickman graduated summa cum laude with a philosophy degree from Kenyon College in Gambier, Ohio. She developed an interest in neuroscience, so she pursued work at a neuroscience laboratory at The University of Illinois at Chicago and spent a year doing graduate work at the Integrated Biomedical Science Program at The Ohio State University. She then attended The Indiana University School of Medicine, from which she graduated with an MD in 2011. Since then, Dr. Hickman has worked as a health, medicine, and science writer, specializing in writing accurately and accessibly about medicine for patients and health science students.

Throughout her career, Dr. Hickman has pursued an interest in education. During college, she volunteered as a tutor at local grade school. Later, during medical school, she volunteered with a group teaching basic medical concepts to fourth- and fifth-grade students, utilizing pictures, props, stories, and tissue samples. She noticed that these students were fascinated with the human body and eager to learn about themselves and how everything fits together.

Dr. Hickman became particularly convinced of the importance of quality patient education in the medical setting. She noticed that patients often had a poor understanding of their own medical conditions, and that this lack of understanding often contributed to poor health outcomes. She is especially excited about this most recent project because it provides her an opportunity to help young people feel comfortable and secure in their bodies. Since many health behaviors are established during adolescence, it provides a unique opportunity to encourage positive health choices over a lifetime.

Dr. Hickman is a member of the American Medical Writers Association. She has served as coauthor or first author on several academic papers. She has written for doctor's offices, patient-education websites, science and medical blogs, and medical education companies such as McGraw-Hill. She can be reached through her website, ruthjhickmanmd.com.

Ruth Jessen Hickman, MD

Contents

About the Author   vi

For Girls   x

- How to Read This Book   x
- What You'll Find in This Book   x
- Special Features   xi

Part One

What is Puberty? What Can I Expect?   1

1 What Is Puberty?   2

- What Changes Can I Expect?   2
- Why Haven't I Started Puberty Yet?   6

2 Changes in Your Body   8

- Will I Really Grow Faster During Puberty?   8
- In What Other Ways Will My Body Change?   9
- How Do I Get Used to My Changing Body?   10

3 Your Period: The Basics   13

- What Is a Period?   13
- Why Do I Have to Get a Period?   14
- Which Reproductive Organs Are on the Outside?   15
- What Is a Menstrual Cycle?   16

4 Hair and Skin Changes   18

- Where Will Hair Changes Occur?   18
- What Is Happening to My Skin?   19
- Why Am I Sweating More?   20

5 Breasts   22

- How Will My Breasts Change?   22
- How Do I Find a Bra That Fits Right?   25
- Breast Q & A with Dr. H   26

Part Two

Health and Hygiene 29

6 Caring For Your Eyes, Mouth, and Ears 30
- Why Do I Need Glasses? 30
- Do I Need to Brush My Teeth More Often? 31
- Can I Really Hurt My Ears? 33

7 Skin Care 35
- What Can I Do About Acne? 35
- What About My Hands and Feet? 40

8 Preventing Body Odor 43
- How Do I Prevent Body Order? 43
- What Are Deodorants and Antiperspirants? 44

9 Hair Care 46
- How Do I Keep My Hair Looking Its Best? 46
- What Do I Do About Body Hair? 49

10 Your Period: What to Do About It 53
- I Got My Period—Now What Do I Do? 53
- What If I Get My Period When I'm Not Expecting It? 56
- What Type of Premenstrual Changes Can I Expect? 58

11 Exercise 60
- What Are the Benefits of Exercise? 60
- Is It Possible to Exercise Too Much? 63

12 Nutrition 65
- What Should I Eat to Stay Healthy? 65
- Dr. H's Guidelines for Healthy Eating 66

13 Sleep 72
- Do My Sleep Needs Change as a Preteen and Teenager? 72
- How Can I Get Enough Sleep? 73

14 Cigarettes, Alcohol and Drugs 76
- What Are the Health Risks of Smoking? 76
- Is Drinking Alcohol Ever Safe? 78
- What Are the Risks of Drugs? 79

Part Three

Your Changing Self: Taking Care of Your Emotions 81

15 Experiencing Highs and Lows 82

- Why Am I Experiencing More Mood Swings? 82
- Why Do My Feelings Seem More Intense? 83

16 Self-Esteem 89

- How Do I Build My Self-Esteem? 89
- How Do I Deal with Bullies? 91

17 School 95

- How Do I Manage New School Stresses? 95
- How Do I Improve in School? 96

18 Friends, Cliques, and Peer Pressure 101

- How Do I Fit In at School? 101
- How Can I Be a Good Friend? 104
- How Do I Handle Peer Pressure? 105

19 Romance and Crushes 108

- Why Do I Like Boys In a Different Way Than I Used To? 108
- What About Breaking Up? 111

20 Parents 112

- Why Is It Harder to Get Along with My Parents? 112
- Do What Is Expected of You 114

21 Discovering Who You Are 117

- Who Do I Want to Be? 117
- How Do I Set Goals for Myself? 121

- Resources 125
- Glossary 127

For Girls

Welcome to *Going through Puberty: A Girl's Manual for Body, Mind, and Health*. I'm Dr. Ruth Hickman, or "Dr. H," as I call myself in this book. I am a medical doctor who writes about health, science, and medicine. I am so excited about this book that I've written for you—young preteen and teenage girls who are or will be going through puberty. It is the kind of book I wish I'd had when I went through these changes myself. It is meant to be a helpful, encouraging resource you can turn to as you go through the ups and downs of puberty. I remember what it was like to go through puberty, but I also talked with many girls about their experiences. Their thoughts are included in this book, too. You should understand that you are not alone. This can be a challenging time, but it is also an exciting time of growth and change.

How to Read This Book

Some of you may be excited to read the information in this book; others may feel nervous or embarrassed. You may feel a combination of emotions. Whatever you are feeling about puberty is totally normal! Take your time with this book. It covers a lot of topics, but you may still have many questions along the way. Don't be afraid to ask the adults in your life these questions.

What You'll Find in This Book

I have divided this book into three parts. In **Part One**, I cover the basic changes you'll be going through during puberty, including getting your period and breast development.

In **Part Two**, I talk about health and hygiene during puberty and beyond. This section provides a lot of tips you can use to keep yourself healthy.

It's not just your body that changes during puberty. Some of the biggest changes are in your emotions, thoughts, and feelings. I talk about these changes in **Part Three**. This section helps you understand these changes and gives you tips for putting together your new social and emotional puzzle.

Special Features

Throughout this book, you will find various special features:

- Boldfaced Key Words with definitions in the Glossary at the end of the book.
- It's a Fact! boxes highlight fun and interesting facts related to each chapter topic.
- Dr. H says provides additional insight or advice from the author.
- Quotes and stories from other preteen and teen girls, and occasionally from their parents, give you insight into others' thoughts and experiences.
- Just For Fun! activities include keeping a journal to track your thoughts and feelings about the many changes you're experiencing.
- Quick Quizzes are sprinkled throughout to "test" your knowledge. Don't worry, these quizzes aren't graded!

During the days ahead, at times you may feel more like a kid, and at other times, you may feel more like a grown-up. You might even feel like both at the same time! Whatever you are feeling, it's normal. It is an amazing time to be you!

Part One

What Is Puberty?
What Can I Expect?

Puberty and **adolescence** are exciting times of growth and change in your body, your brain, and your mind. Puberty is a normal phase of development that occurs when a child's body transitions into an adult's body and becomes capable of reproduction. In this section, you'll learn about what puberty is, and the changes you can expect to take place in your body, brain, and even your emotions. Later in this book, you'll learn what you can do to make yourself more comfortable with all these changes.

What Is Puberty?

Let's answer your questions...

- What Changes Can I Expect?
- Why Haven't I Started Puberty Yet?

What Changes Can I Expect?

Congratulations! You are beginning a new and exciting time in your life: **puberty**. Puberty is an exciting time of growth and change in your body, brain, and emotions.

Your Body

During puberty, your body will change in many different ways. This may seem strange. But these changes take place over months and years, so you'll have time to get used to it.

Body Changes

- Breasts start to develop.
- Periods begin.
- Height quickly increases, then stops (called a **growth spurt**).
- Hair will appear in places there wasn't hair before.
- Skin and hair may become oily.
- Sweat will have an odor.

It's a Fact!

Hormones

Hormones are signaling molecules, special chemicals released into the bloodstream that travel all around your body. They help control how cells and organs work. While there are many different hormones in the body, two groups of hormones are particularly important for your development both before birth and during puberty: **estrogens** and androgens. I call estrogens "girl hormones" because girls have more of these hormones in their bodies. (Boys have more androgens.) The hormone differences trigger the various changes that occur as girls and boys mature into women and men.

Your Brain

You probably know that your brain helps you think and feel. But did you know that even your brain changes during puberty?

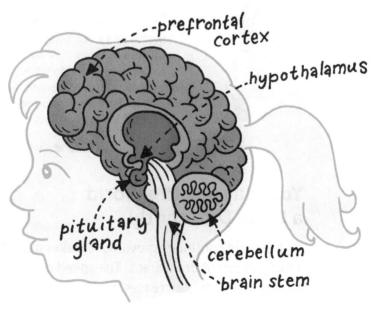

prefrontal cortex

hypothalamus

pituitary gland

cerebellum

brain stem

Preteens and teens tend to:

- Respond to situations, especially emotional situations, more on feeling and intuition, while adults are more likely to use reason.
- Have more difficulty planning for the future than adults, although they are better at this than when they were children.
- Experience an increased drive for new and dramatic sensations. This is fine when the exciting experience is a safe one, like riding a roller coaster, but it can be problematic if the new sensation is unsafe.
- Find it harder to control that fun impulse and exchange it for a calm, logical look at the long-terms risks of a situation.

Dr. H says: "One area of the brain that develops a lot during your preteen and teen years is the prefrontal cortex. This area is important for controlling impulses, moderating emotions with logic, and planning for the future. It won't fully mature until you are well into your twenties!"

Changes in Social Interactions

During puberty, parts of the brain involved in social interaction become more complex. Not only do social interactions become more complicated, but you also might become more sensitive to rejection by your peers. You might feel more self-conscious, and you might have more mood swings. All of this is related to developmental changes in certain areas of the brain.

" Ooooo, I get so irritated and annoyed sometimes, and I don't know why. One day my aunt told me that it is really normal for girls to feel just like I do when they are going through puberty. She said I shouldn't feel bad about it. That made me feel so much better. But I still get irritated sometimes!"

Diane age 12

You May See the World a Little Differently

As the brain continues growing, it makes more connections among different brain areas. The speed of the connections among brain areas increases, too, contributing to more complex and abstract thoughts. You get better at looking at one situation and seeing how it is related to other situations. As you get older, you start to understand that not everything is "right" or "wrong," but that many situations are somewhere in between.

Ooooo! Brain freeze! I hope that doesn't stop my brain from growing!

Very funny! I'm pretty sure the cold ice cream is not going to stop your brain from growing.

Stay Flexible Even If Your Brain Is Less Flexible

At the same time the brain is growing, it is starting to lose some of its flexibility. For example, some things are easier to learn as a child than as an adult, like languages. It is probably easier for you to learn a new language than it is for your mom or dad. This flexibility is one of the advantages of youth. You are still in the process of developing your self-identity, so it's easier for you to change than it is for adults.

Your Brain Doesn't "Make You" Do Anything!

It's important to understand that your brain doesn't "make you" do things. You always have a choice about how to respond to a situation. Knowing more about yourself and about how you are changing can help you make better decisions as you grow into adulthood!

" I don't like it when I feel like crying, or I feel really irritated, and I don't know why. I even snapped at my mom when she was trying to help. She told me it was just puberty. I told her not to use that word. I don't know if I want help. Sometimes I just want to be left alone to figure it out. My mom said that is perfectly okay. She said if I want to talk to her I can, and if I don't, that's okay, too. That made me feel better, and I talked to her for a long time."

Madeline age 11

Why Haven't I Started Puberty Yet?

Puberty happens at a different time for every girl. Once it starts, girls also differ in how long the process takes. This variation is normal. Just like some girls have blue eyes, and others have brown eyes, some girls go through puberty earlier, and others go through it later. Your body's timing is your own. Trust it!

Dr. H says: "In a few rare cases, girls start maturing very early or very late due to medical reasons. This is extremely unusual, though, and nothing you should worry about."

Puberty Myths

You can't act like a kid anymore.

You will suddenly be all grown up.

All these changes will happen at the same time.

Your body will be out of control.

Your emotions will always feel extreme.

Your body will not change all at once, and you won't become a totally different person overnight. Don't worry if you sometimes feel like your inside and outside don't match. They will catch up with each other over time. Everyone experiences puberty a little differently. So don't compare yourself to your friends, your older sister, or your cousin. There is no "right" age to get a bra or start wearing deodorant—wait until the time is right for you.

Quick Quiz
. . . .
Every girl who goes through puberty becomes overly emotional and irritable. True or False?

Just For Fun!

Journaling

You may already keep a journal or diary, or you may even do journaling in school. Why not start a journal that's just for your thoughts and feelings about growing up? Keeping a journal is a fun way to keep track of the changes you're going through. There is no right or wrong way to keep a journal. There are suggestions throughout this book, but you should feel free to put whatever you'd like in your journal. You may want to write, draw pictures, or include poems or articles you like. You can also cut out words, phrases, and pictures from magazines and paste them into your journal. All you need to get started is a notebook or loose-leaf paper in a binder and a pen or pencil. You may also want to use colored pencils, markers, crayons, a glue stick or tape, and old magazines or newspapers.

Start your journal by writing down 10 (or more) things you really love about yourself. Then pick one of the things you wrote down and write a few sentences about why you chose it. You might even want to include a picture of yourself. Have fun with this!

Changes in Your Body

Let's talk about changes in your body...

- Will I Really Grow Faster During Puberty?
- In What Other Ways Will My Body Change?
- How Do I Get Used to My Changing Body?

Will I Really Grow Faster During Puberty?

You've been gradually growing during your childhood. You may have experienced a few smaller growth spurts, but during puberty you really start growing. For girls, growth starts to pick up around age 9. Many girls grow the fastest around age 11 or 12. But remember, the exact age varies! When you are growing at your peak rate, you may grow over three inches a year. Most girls hit the fastest part of their growth spurt just *before* they start having periods. (You'll learn all about periods on pp.13-17.) After your growth spurt is over, you will probably only grow about two or three more inches. By about age 15, most girls reach their adult height.

> **I am the only girl in my class with breasts, and I feel totally embarrassed every day. My science teacher heard one of the boys tease me. After class, she told that she had developed early just like me. She said my hormones were in a hurry and everyone else's would catch up. She said I should be proud to be me no matter what."**
>
> Savannah age 10

Body Parts Grow at Different Rates

During puberty, you might notice that not all of your body parts grow at the same rate. Your head doesn't grow much at all during puberty. Some parts of your body grow really fast, like your feet, arms, legs, and spine. What's funny is that your feet usually grow fastest first, then your arms and legs, and finally your spine. This can feel awkward for a while, but it's normal. It will all even out in the end.

It's a Fact!

Girls tend to get their growth spurt a couple of years before boys, which is why preteen girls often find themselves towering over the boys in their class. But boys grow faster once they hit their growth spurt, and they keep growing longer than girls.

In What Other Ways Will My Body Change?

During puberty, you don't just get taller—your body shape changes, too. Some of your bones, like your hip bones, grow into a slightly different shape. This will give your body some curves that you didn't have when you were younger. Also contributing to your changing body shape is more **adipose tissue**, or fat, also contributes to your changing body shape. Before puberty ramps up, you might notice some extra fat on your belly, but a lot of this fat will move to your hips, thighs, and breasts. It's a normal and healthy part of development for girls to add weight quickly before adding much height.

It's a Fact!

Increasing amounts of hormones called estrogens trigger all the changes you experience during puberty.

Changes to Your "Private Parts"

What we often refer to as our "private parts" are really our reproductive organs, such as the vagina, uterus, cervix, ovaries, and fallopian tubes. Changes in your reproductive organs may be less noticeable to you than other physical changes, but these organs change in shape and size, too.

How Do I Get Used to My Changing Body?

It's normal to want to look and feel your best. As you go through puberty, and even as you become an adult, you might start focusing more on your outer appearance. This is normal! But sometimes this can get out of whack. You might begin to think too much about a single physical characteristic that you may consider a "flaw." It can be easy to give this flaw exaggerated importance and become overly concerned about it. It's common to focus on parts of ourselves that others don't even notice.

Dr. H says: "Remember, all of these changes happen according to your own inner timing. There is no reason to worry if you are a little later or earlier than the average. Your body knows exactly what to do for you!"

Images from magazines, television, and movies can make this even harder, because they often project unrealistic views of how girls should look. So it isn't surprising girls can get the idea that the way they look is more important than who they are. This simply isn't true. Your inner qualities—like how you treat your friends, your kindness toward others, and your hard work—are more important than how you look on the outside. If you find yourself too focused on parts of your appearance that you don't like, try to remember what matters most: who you are as a person. Celebrate who you are as a person and accept yourself as you are.

It might take you while to get used to the changes in your body shape. It's common for some girls to think they have become "fat" when they haven't. Your curves are beautiful! But they wouldn't be possible without the extra body fat you gain in your preteen and teen years. No matter what your body shape, don't assume you are overweight. It's true that some girls weigh more than they should, based on their height. Others girls weigh less than they should. An unhealthy weight—whether it is too high or too low—can lead to serious health problems. If you are concerned about

Dr. H says: "Throughout history, certain kinds of 'beauty' have gone in and out of fashion. You might notice that one year, curly hair is in fashion, and the next year it's straight hair. Think about how silly it is to change who you are every time a magazine says you should. You don't have to change anything about yourself to be beautiful."

"Girls, you are unique. There is no one else in the entire world just like you. What makes you so special is who you are on the inside. You are not supposed to look like that girl or woman in the magazine any more than the girl in the magazine is supposed to look like you. Look like yourself, be yourself, love yourself. You make this world a special place because there is only one of you!"

Kathleen, mother of three

your weight, talk to your doctor. He or she will be able to take into account your age, your weight, and your stage of puberty to give you an accurate view of your developing body. If you are eating in an unhealthy way, your doctor will give you suggestions to help.

Deceptive Images of Beauty

It's easy to get caught up in the images of women and girls who you see in the media. It's important to keep in mind that these women have professional makeup artists, hair stylists, and designers working together to make them look so good. Often the images in magazines are altered by computers. Certain computer programs can remove wrinkles or pimples, and can even make women look thinner. So don't compare yourself to these images. They usually aren't real. Sometimes, if you look too many of these distorted images, you can get the idea that looks are more important than who you are on the inside. Remember, that's not true!

It can be especially upsetting to look at these images during a time when your body is changing so much. Remember that beauty comes in many forms. If there are parts of your appearance that you don't like, focus on others that you do like. Or focus and abilities that give you self-confidence, like being good at athletics or art, being a gifted student, being a funny person, or being a good friend. We all have special gifts and talents to offer, and they have nothing to do with our outward appearance.

Just For Fun!

Make a "Beautiful Girls and Women" Collage

Gather pictures from magazines and newspapers, photographs of your friends and family, and even images of women from history. Choose images based on who these women are on the inside, not what they look like. After you make your collage, write down some key words that describe why these women are beautiful. For example, if you choose a photo of your grandmother, you might write down "loving," "kind," and "great at cooking."

3 Your Period: The Basics

Let's answer your questions...

- What Is a Period?
- Why Do I Have to Get a Period?
- Which Reproductive Organs Are on the Outside?
- What Is a Menstrual Cycle?

What Is a Period?

Getting your period is a process called **menstruation**. This process is called "getting your period" or "that time of the month" because it happens "periodically," about once every month. The first time a girl has her period is called her **menarche**. In the United States, the average age for a girl to start her period is 12, but this can vary widely. You might be between 9 and 16 when you start your period.

It's a Fact!

The average age girls start their period is younger than it used to be. In 1900, the average age of menarche in the United States was about 14. Currently, it is 12. Scientists aren't quite sure why, but they think it is partly due to better nutrition.

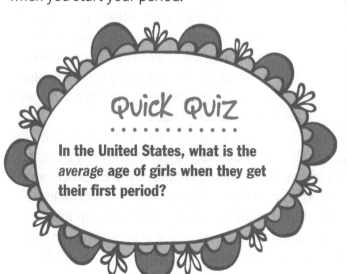

Quick Quiz

In the United States, what is the *average* age of girls when they get their first period?

Why Do I Have to Get a Period?

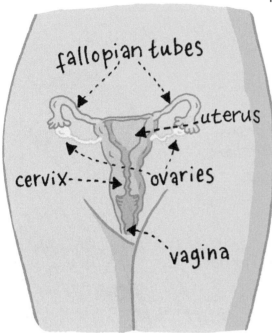

Female reproductive organs

To better understand this, let's take a quick tour of your internal reproductive organs. First is the **vagina**, the muscular tubular structure that leads to the **vaginal opening**. The bigger open space that connects to the vagina is called the uterus. It looks like an upside-down triangle. The tip of the triangle-shaped **uterus** is called the **cervix**. The uterus has two hollow, arm-like structures coming out from it. These are called **fallopian tubes**. The other ends of the fallopian tubes open to the inside of your body. Attached to the uterus are two other structures that look like thin lines leading to two ovals. These oval areas are the **ovaries**. You have one on each side of your body.

The Ovaries

The ovaries are a very important part of the female reproductive system for two reasons. First, most of the estrogens ("girl hormones") in a female's body are produced in the ovaries. As you progress through puberty, your ovaries mature. They start releasing more and more estrogens, until they reach the level of an adult woman. These increases in estrogens trigger many other changes in your body, including your growth spurt and breast development.

Second, the ovaries are the areas that store the special cells called **ova**, or "eggs." (A single egg cell is called an ovum.) In older girls and mature women, an ovum bursts out of the ovary about once a month in a process called **ovulation**. The ovum then floats up into the fallopian tube and eventually into the uterus. When there is no pregnancy, the ovum just falls apart after a while. Once

An ovum bursts out of the ovary about once a month in a process called ovulation.

you are on a regular cycle, the ovary releases an ovum about two weeks before menstruation. You will probably have your first ovulation (release of an ovum) around the same time you get your first period. Once you start having periods, you will probably not ovulate regularly right away, but you will eventually.

Which Reproductive Organs Are on the Outside?

The external reproductive organs are the ones on the outside of your body. Because of where they are located, your external reproductive organs can be a little hard to visualize. If you want, you can try and identify these organs on yourself with the help of a mirror. The general name for this whole region is the **vulva**.

The vulva has several different parts, all with different names. The **mons** (or **mons pubis**) refers to the soft, slightly raised area over the pubic bone. It is the area where pubic hair first starts to appear. In the outer region of the vulva you can see a fold of skin on the left and right side. These are called the **outer lips** (or **labia majora**). Unless the legs are spread apart, the outer lips come together to protect the rest of the genitals. Inside the outer lips are smaller and thinner folds, one on each side. These are called the **inner lips** (or **labia minora**). Together, the inner lips and outer lips are called the **labia**. Near the top, the inner lips join to form a sort of hood. Peeking out from under this hood is an organ called the **clitoris**, which is a very sensitive area. Inside the inner lips is the **vaginal opening**, which opens into your **vagina**. This is the space inside the body that leads to the rest of your internal reproductive organs. You might not be able to see the vaginal opening, but it's there. Most girls also have a thin layer covering most or part of the vaginal opening. This area is called the **hymen**, but you probably won't be able to see it either. This area is usually stretched over time.

It's a Fact!

During puberty, your ovaries and fallopian tubes enlarge, and your uterus grows. The uterus is the place where a new human begins to form when a woman becomes pregnant. When your uterus has grown to its adult size, it will be about the size of a pear, but it gets bigger when a baby is growing inside.

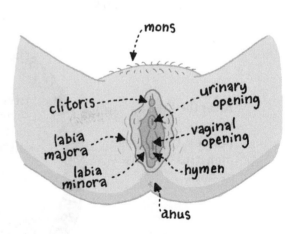

mons

clitoris

urinary opening

labia majora

vaginal opening

labia minora

hymen

anus

One place you will start to see new hair growth is on your vulva.

What Is a Menstrual Cycle?

It's a Fact!

Your estrogens from your ovaries are responsible for the monthly cyclical changes that lead to your period. The blood and tissue you see when you get your period actually comes from the lining inside your uterus. Your menstrual cycle begins on the first day you start bleeding and lasts until the next time you start bleeding. The average cycle is 28 days, but it's normal to have a cycle as short as 21 days or as long as 35 days. When you first start to menstruate, you probably won't have a regular cycle. It might be a couple months before you have another period, or it might be less than 28 days. Over time, your cycle should become more predictable, but this may take two or three years.

Having Your Period Doesn't Hurt

You might think this process sounds a little scary. After all, when you think of blood, you probably think of injury and pain. The actual bleeding that takes place when you get your period doesn't hurt. However, sometimes the symptoms that come with your period are uncomfortable. You might feel more tired or get mild cramps. Suggestions for making yourself more comfortable during your period appear on p.58.

After the first 2-3 years of getting periods, the average menstrual cycle is 28 days.

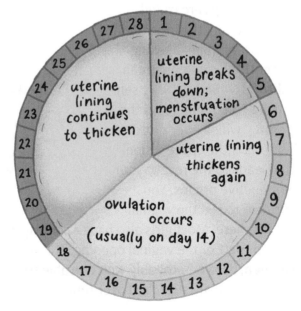

More Period Facts

- The blood from your period might be pink, red, or brown. It can be liquid only or liquid with clots or clumps.
- A period usually lasts between two and six days, with heavier bleeding in the earlier days.
- All girls and women of a certain age range menstruate, unless they are taking certain medications, have certain medical issues, are pregnant, or have just had a baby.
- When you get your period, you might shed between one-quarter to one-third cup of blood and other tissue out through your vagina. This happens over the course of *several* days.

Quick Quiz

Every girl has the same cycle for her period, and it lasts the same number of days. True or False?

Just For Fun!

Talk About It

Take some time to talk to the women in your family about their experience with their period. How old were they when they had their first period? Did anyone tell them what to expect? I bet you can come up with a lot of other questions to ask. Your mom or other family members will likely be happy to share their experiences with you, and if you feel like it, you can talk about your feelings, too.

4 Hair and Skin Changes

Let's talk about hair and skin changes...

- **Where Will Hair Changes Occur?**
- **What Is Happening to My Skin?**
- **Why Am I Sweating More?**

Where Will Hair Changes Occur?

Other changes you'll see have to do with your hair. The hair on your head may change in thickness, texture, or color, and it may become oily.

Many girls notice their hair is oilier in their preteen and teen years than it was when they were younger. This is due to increased activity of **sebaceous glands**, tiny glands in the skin. These sebaceous glands release **sebum**, an oily substance that flows out onto the skin. Sebum is important to protect your skin and hair. But sometimes your body produces too much of it, and it ends up on your scalp. When this happens, many girls start washing their hair more often, which can help.

Quick Quiz

The texture or color of your hair may change during adolescence. True or False?

Changes in Body Hair

You will also start to see hair grow in places you didn't have it before. Hair starts to grow on a private part of your body called your vulva. The hair that grows here is called **pubic hair**. There is a lot of variety in what this hair looks like. It often starts out thin and light-colored, but over time it usually becomes curlier and darker than the hair on your head.

Hair will also start to grow under your armpits, and the hair on your forearms and legs might get thicker and darker. Some girls notice slight hair growth on their upper lip, too. Girls differ a great deal in the color, length, and thickness of the hair in these areas. This hair growth is perfectly natural, and it's nothing to feel embarrassed about. It's just another sign that your body is maturing.

What Is Happening to My Skin?

The increased sebum released by sebaceous glands also increases oiliness of the skin. In many cases, this leads to **acne**. Acne includes **pimples** (also called "zits"), which are large, inflamed, raised regions that are sore to the touch.

Most young people experience at least a little acne at some point during adolescence. For girls, the peak time for acne is about age 14. The most common locations for acne are on your face, neck, chest, and back. On your face, acne tends to be worse on your forehead, nose, and chin (called the "T-zone") because this area has the most sebaceous glands.

> " I had acne on my back, and it was really bad. My mom kept saying I was lucky I didn't have it on my face, but I didn't feel lucky at all. I hated changing my shirt for gym because I was so embarrassed. Finally, my doctor told me to get a back scrubber for the shower, and use it every day with a special soap. It really helped a lot."
>
> Tanya age 13

Dr. **H** says: "Almost everybody has to deal with acne at some point in his or her life. But there are many effective treatments. Later in the book you'll find tips for how to handle it."

Quick Quiz

You can only get acne on your face. True or False?

Why Am I Sweating More?

Sweating is an important way to keep cool. Once you enter puberty, a special kind of sweat gland is activated. These sweat glands release the type of sweat bacteria love. These bacteria don't hurt you in any way, but they do produce a waste product with a distinct smell that we call "body odor" or "B.O." Body odor is a natural and normal consequence of this cooling process. The funny thing is that you might not even notice your own odor, since it starts gradually, and you are always around the smell. But you might notice someone else's!

Dr. H says: "There is wide cultural variability about how much body odor is considered acceptable. In the United States, people tend to be very anti–body odor. But in many countries around the world, it is not such a big deal."

Just For Fun!

Freshen Up Your Routine

Get a piece of paper and write out your "Stay Fresh" routine. Start in the morning and go through your day. Your list might include things like these:

1. Shower and wash with soap and washcloth.
2. Put on deodorant.
3. Moisturize with body lotion.
4. Stock gym bag with deodorant, washcloth, portable soap, and fresh change of clothes.
5. Shower after activities like basketball, dance, or soccer.
6. Wash face and use any acne products needed.

Write your list on your paper, and post it where you can see it every day.

5 Breasts

Let's answer your questions...

- How Will My Breasts Change?
- How Do I Find a Bra That Fits Right?
- Breast Q & A with Dr. H

How Will My Breasts Change?

Girls tend to have different feelings about their growing breasts. Some girls are excited about it; others don't pay much attention. Some girls feel self-conscious if they start to develop earlier than other girls; others worry they aren't developing fast enough. Every girl's body has its own inner timing for these changes. There is nothing you can do to speed up or slow down the process.

Five Stages of Breast Development

There are typically five stages of breast development.

Stage 1: This is the stage before a girl starts puberty. The **nipples** rise off the chest a little, but otherwise the chest is flat. There are **areolas**, the darker colored areas which surround the nipple, but they are small. At this stage, boys' and girls' breasts do not differ much.

Stage 2: This is the earliest stage of development during puberty. Some girls reach this phase when they are only 7 or 8, and others might not get there until they're 13. The average age is between 8 and 11 years old. During this stage, the areolas start to get bigger. Something called a "breast bud" forms underneath the nipple. It might feel hard and lumpy, and it will start to make the nipple stick out from the chest. The development of breast buds is one of the most common first signs of puberty in girls.

Stage 3: During this stage, the areolas continue to enlarge, and they start to elevate even more. The nipples get larger, too. The age for this stage varies, but ranges from about 9 to 13. The average age for girls to reach this stage is 11 or 12.

Stage 4: This is the last stage of breast development before the fully mature state. At this stage, the nipple and areola form a separate mound that sticks out from the rest of the breast. The areola and nipple continue to enlarge. Some girls skip this stage entirely and go straight to Stage 5. Girls usually enter this stage between ages 10 and 15, and the average age is 12 or 13.

Stage 5: Breasts are considered fully developed at this stage, although some girls' breasts get larger after they have entered this stage. This is when the nipple and areola have formed a continuous line with the rest of the breast. This stage occurs anytime between ages 12 and 18. A girl usually reaches Stage 5 four or five years after she starts developing.

Dr. H says: "Human beings are mammals. Like other mammals, their anatomy allows them to breast-feed their young. That's the real reason females have breasts."

Breast Soreness

Some girls notice some soreness to their breasts as their breasts are growing. This is almost never something you need to worry about, but you can always tell your doctor about it if you are concerned.

Breast Size

Size alone is not a good indicator of breast maturity. Some girls have relatively small breasts, and others have larger breasts. It's the same for adult women. The age when you start to develop breasts does not affect the breast size you'll have as a grown woman.

How Do I Find a Bra That Fits Right?

How do you get a fabulous fit?

1. **Get out a measuring tape.** Bras are sized by band size and cup size. To find your band size, measure around your rib cage, right below your breast (where the band of the bra would be). Keep the measuring tape tight around you. If possible, get help from your mom, a sister, or even a professional bra fitter. If you get a half number (such as 29½), round up (30).

   Next, measure your cup size, which is represented by one or more letters. To do this, you can measure your naked breast or you can measure your chest with a bra already on. You'll want to measure loosely this time around the fullest part of your breasts. Take the number you get for your cup size measurement and subtract the number you got for the band size. The difference between these numbers will give you your cup size, as shown in the chart below.

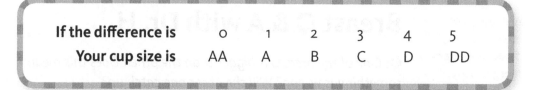

If the difference is	0	1	2	3	4	5
Your cup size is	AA	A	B	C	D	DD

2. **Talk to a professional.** This measurement is just a starting point. There can be a lot of variations in sizes depending on the brand you're buying. So your best bet might be to talk to a professional bra fitter.

3. **Your size will change.** As you grow and change, your breast size will change, too. You'll want to check your measurements periodically to make sure you have the best fit.

Dr. H says: "Some girls want to wear a bra even if they haven't developed much yet. That's fine! Before bringing it up with a parent, you might want to think about why you want a bra. You might explain that your breasts are more sensitive now that they are starting to develop, or maybe that you feel self-conscious without one. Perhaps you want to get used to wearing one now, or maybe you want a bra to show that you are growing up. Maybe all of your friends have bras, and you don't want to be left out. Just be honest about it."

Bra Types

There are various types of bras, too. Training bras are designed for girls whose breasts are just starting to develop. That's the kind of bra many girls start with, but you may be beyond that stage when you get your first bra.

❝ I'm so excited to have my first bra that I wear it all day and sleep in it, too. I have three bras in different colors. I feel proud and happy about how I look!"

Bonnie age 12

It's a Fact!

Did you know that 80 percent of women wear the wrong bra size?

It's a Fact!

Training bras were first marketed to girls in the 1950s. Before that time, developing girls wore camisoles, which are sleeveless undergarments.

Breast Q & A with Dr. H

Q: *One of my breasts is bigger than the other. Does this mean something is wrong? Will the other one catch up?*

A: While your breasts are developing, it's very common for one breast to be ahead of the other in development and thus larger. This often evens out by the time you stop growing, but most women have at least a slight difference in the size of their breasts. It's unlikely anyone else can notice the size difference between your breasts. If you are really self-conscious about it, you can wear a bra insert on one side. But really, having one breast that's slightly larger than the other is normal and nothing to worry about!

Q: *My breasts are pretty big already and they make me feel self-conscious. What can I do?*

A: You are not alone! Many girls who have large breasts feel the same way you do—especially when their breasts have just recently developed. It can take a while to get used to your growing breasts. Wear a bra that fits right, or get a new one that fits your growing size. Don't let this undermine your self-confidence. People can only make you self-conscious if you let them. Be proud of your beautiful body!

Q: *My breasts are so small. I am ready for them to grow already! Is there anything I can do to speed them up?*

A: There are many girls who feel like you do, but there really isn't anything you can do to speed up the process. Your breasts are on their own schedule and will grow according to your unique set of genetic instructions! You can do exercises to tone the layer of muscle underneath the breast. This can make your breasts *look* more defined, but it won't make your breasts grow more quickly or get larger.

Your breasts will look larger if you have good posture. Sit with your shoulders down and back instead of slumped forward. Remember, some adult women have small breasts even though their breasts are fully developed. Whether you are large breasted, small breasted, or somewhere in between, part of growing into a woman is learning to accept and love yourself just as you are! Be patient and positive!

Q: *My breasts are still small, and I can feel a lump in my breast just underneath the nipple. It's sort of tender. I don't notice one on the other side. Is this normal? I'm 10 years old. My aunt had cancer, and she had a lump in her breast.*

A: What you have described is probably a breast bud, an early sign of breast development. It's composed of newly forming breast tissue. It's very common to have a breast bud on one side but not the other. The lumpy feeling will go away eventually. Often this area is a little sensitive or sore. Breast cancer is very, very rare in girls your age. But you can always have your doctor check it out. It's great that you are so aware of the changes happening in your body!

Quick Quiz

It is very common for one of your breasts to be slightly larger than the other. True or False?

Just For Fun!

Your Changing Body

Take out your journal and spend some time writing, drawing, or even cutting out words or pictures from magazines to describe your feelings about your breasts and any thoughts you have about their development. Try to be kind and positive toward your body. Keep in mind all the amazing work your body is doing as you grow into a woman! Write down three things you love about your body. Maybe it's that you can run fast, that you like the color of your eyes, or that you have pretty hands. Whatever it is, write it down. Write a sentence or two about why you love that part of yourself and why you are grateful for it.

Part Two

Health and Hygiene

ow you know about the most significant changes that happen in your body during puberty. In this section, I'll give you the information you need to deal with these changes effectively. As you grow up, you'll need to keep doing some things you are already doing to take care of yourself. But you may need to add to or modify your behaviors and routines. We'll also talk about some of the most important things you'll need to do to protect and promote your health as a preteen and beyond. Now that you're growing up, you're taking on even more responsibility for your health. The good habits you create now will take you into a healthy future!

6 Caring for Your Eyes, Teeth, and Ears

Let's answer your questions...

- Why Do I Need Glasses?
- Do I Need to Brush My Teeth More Often?
- Can I Really Hurt My Ears?

Why Do I Need Glasses?

Vision problems become more common as girls become preteens and teenagers. During your growth spurt, your eyes grow very quickly, and sometimes one part of the eye grows out of proportion to the rest of the eye. When that happens, the eye can't properly focus on an image.

Changes in your eyesight often happen gradually, so you may not immediately notice a difference in your ability to see well. If you are having trouble making out objects, mention this to your parents, so you can get your eyes checked. Headaches or double vision are other signs that you may need to get an eye exam.

> "I had trouble seeing the board from the back of the classroom, but I didn't want to tell anyone because I didn't want to get glasses. Then one day my teacher asked me to read what she had written on the board, and I couldn't. I was so embarrassed to have to get glasses. But getting glasses wasn't so bad. I got some that actually look really cool, and some of the kids said they wished they could wear glasses, too!"
>
> *Stacie* age 10

Glasses

If you do have an issue with your vision, it usually isn't a big deal. Depending on your age, you will probably need either glasses or contacts. You may feel shy or upset about having to wear glasses. This is natural feeling. It may take some time to get used to them, but you will. Glasses are convenient to wear. All you need to keep them working great is a good lens cleaner. You can usually wear glasses comfortably while you are playing sports or being active outdoors.

Contacts

Contacts are another option for some people with vision issues. If you wear contacts, you have to be very responsible about taking care of them. Contacts can irritate or even infect your eyes if they are not cleaned regularly. If you do get contacts, be sure to follow all of your eye doctor's instructions.

Dr. H says: "If you feel like you are ready for the responsibility of contacts, you can mention to your parents that some contacts give sharper overall vision and sharper peripheral (side) vision than glasses. Some types may even help keep your eyesight from getting worse."

Protecting Your Eyes from the Sun

Even if you don't need glasses or contacts, every girl should invest in at least one pair of glasses—sunglasses! Even though your eyes can't get a sunburn like your skin can, radiation from the sun can damage your eyes. Look for cool shades that provide UVA/UVB protection. The sunglasses you choose do not have to be expensive to be effective.

Do I Need to Brush My Teeth More Often?

Just like when you were younger, you should brush your teeth at least twice a day. Your parents probably don't supervise your brushing the way they used to, so now it's up

to you to do a great job even when no one is checking. That's part of growing up!

Pick a toothbrush with soft bristles, and make sure you replace it every few months. Dentists recommend toothpastes with fluoride to help prevent tooth decay. You can experiment with different brands of toothpaste to find one you like. Don't brush too hard! This can actually damage your teeth or gums. Hold your toothbrush at an angle to your gums. Make sure you brush the whole surface of every single tooth—it will take a few minutes. Don't forget to brush your tongue, too.

It is also important to floss daily. Flossing properly isn't hard, and your dentist can show you how to do it. While brushing and flossing daily can help prevent tooth decay and cavities, you should also avoid or limit your intake of sugary foods and drinks. Mouthwash with fluoride can provide extra protection if you are prone to cavities, and it helps keep your breath fresh.

It's a Fact!

Sugarless gum may help prevent tooth decay. It does this by removing plaque and other debris from your teeth as you chew.

Braces and Retainers

If your teeth grow in at the wrong angle or with improper spacing, you may need to have this corrected. Most of the time, this means getting a retainer, braces, or both. Retainers are used either before braces are put on your teeth or after your braces are removed.

Caring for Your Braces

It's easy for tooth decay to start behind your braces if you don't keep them really clean. So it's extra important to brush your teeth after every meal and snack. It's even more important to floss your teeth regularly. Avoid hard or sticky foods that can break your braces.

Keep Smiling

If you have to get braces, remember that they're temporary. In the meantime, use having braces as an opportunity to take really good care of your teeth. Remember, braces don't change the wonderful person you are on the inside.

Can I Really Hurt My Ears?

Dr. H says: "Don't forget to take care of your ears, too! Don't listen to your music too loud, with or without earbuds or headphones. Over time, listening to very loud music can damage your hearing. If you can't hear what is going on around you while you are listening to music, turn down the volume! Also, even though it's tempting, don't stick anything inside your ears—not even a cotton swab. It's easy to puncture your eardrum that way. Finally, if you get your ears pierced, be sure to follow any instructions you get for keeping them clean. That will help minimize chances of infection."

It's a Fact!

Pierced ears have been found in human remains from 5,000 years ago. It's an old tradition!

Just For Fun!

Establish a New, Healthy Habit

It can take a while to establish new habits. Take some time to think about what healthy, new habit you want to establish for yourself. You may have more than one. When you choose a new habit, first write it down in your journal. (For example, "I want to start flossing every day.") Then, make a plan for how you are going to establish this new habit. Reward yourself when you follow through with your new habit for a whole week!

7 Skin Care

Let's talk about skin care...

- **What Can I Do About Acne?**
- **What About My Hands and Feet?**

What Can I Do About Acne?

Many preteens and teens struggle with acne. If you're one of them, you're not alone. Acne is highly treatable. If you are having problems with acne, first try the changes I suggest below. Give them a couple of months to work. If you are not satisfied with your results, see your family physician or a dermatologist (a doctor who specializes in skin problems). There are many effective treatments for acne your doctor can

Dr. H says: "If you are having trouble with very severe acne, you should see your doctor. There is no need to wait!"

There are three skin care basics:

1. Clean
2 Treat
3. Protect

prescribe. You don't have to suffer with acne. With good skin care and the help of your doctor, you can go through your teen years feeling happy in your own skin!

Clean

Keeping your skin clean is a good place to start.

- Gently clean your face twice a day with a mild facial cleanser. There is no need to clean it more often than that. You can do this in the morning and evening. This will help wash away extra oil as well as dirt or makeup.

- Find a cleanser that says "noncomedogenic" or "nonacnegenic," which just means it won't aggravate acne.

- There is no need to use a harsh scrub.

- Use a gentle body wash or soap when you take a shower or bath and after you exercise.

Now that your face is clean, you'll want to try to keep it that way. If you have bangs, make sure you keep your hair clean, too. Oily hair and hair products on the skin can aggravate acne. Avoid tight-fitting hats or headbands, which can trap sweat, oil, and dirt. The same principle applies to body acne (usually on your chest or back), so avoid tight-fitting or dirty clothes. Change your pillowcase once a week. Also, try to avoid touching your face unless you have just washed your hands.

Treat

You can skip this step if acne isn't a problem for you. If it is, you'll want to apply some sort of treatment, usually after you wash your face. You can also buy a facial soap and body wash that contains one of these products, so you can clean and treat all at once.

- Start with an over-the-counter treatment. The most common products contain **benzoyl peroxide** or **salicylic acid**.

- Benzoyl peroxide works to kill the bacteria associated with acne formation. It is better than salicylic acid for treating pimples (acne that is red and puffy).

- Salicylic acid helps prevent clogged **hair follicles** and clean out follicles that are already plugged.

It can take a while for your skin to get used to these medications, so go slowly. They may cause your skin to be drier than usual. You'll want to buy a product you can use over your whole face (and any other area of the body where you have acne). You can also buy "spot treatments," which are usually more concentrated, to treat a painful, inflamed pimple. Some people have successfully used a combination of these products. Pick one product to start with until you see how your skin adjusts. If your skin has not cleared up after a couple of months, see your doctor.

Dr. H says: "Some people are sensitive to products with benzoyl peroxide or salicylic acid. So before using it on your face, apply the treatment to a small region of skin to make sure you aren't sensitive or allergic. Follow all instructions on the package carefully. If you use too much too fast, you may make your skin worse."

Protect

Protection is the final step for beautiful skin. You can protect yourself from the sun's radiation by wearing sunscreen every day. Over time, sun exposure can cause premature wrinkling, and it increases the risk of skin cancer. Skin cancer is the most common cancer in the United States, and it is the highest cancer risk for Americans 15 to 39 years old. Apply a layer of sunscreen every day after you wash your face and

apply any acne treatment products. (If you wear makeup, put it on after you put on sunscreen.)

The easiest way to apply sunscreen is to use a moisturizing lotion that has sunscreen in it. This way, you moisturize and protect your skin all at once. Some over-the-counter acne medications and certain kinds of prescribed acne medications may dry out the skin, making moisturizer and sunscreen use even more important. Pick a sunscreen that says "full spectrum protection" or "protects against UVA and UVB rays."

Extended Protection

Of course, if you plan on getting extended sun, you'll need to apply sunscreen all over your body. Here are some tips for caring for your skin when you're in the sun:

- Don't forget to use a lip balm with SPF to protect your lips.
- Although the sun's rays are most damaging between 10 a.m. and 4 p.m., you need protection at other times of the day, too. You even need it in the winter and when it's cloudy.
- Use an SPF of at least 15. I recommend SPF 30, especially if you have fair skin.

- Make sure you use generous amounts of sunscreen, and reapply it often. Most people don't use enough sunscreen, so really slather it on any part of your body that will be exposed to the sun.
- Using additional protection like clothing and hats is a great idea, too.

Don't be fooled into thinking tanning is a safe way to get some sun. While it is true that a gentle tan is easier on your skin than a sunburn, even a tan damages your skin and increases your risk of skin cancer. In other words, there is no such thing as a safe tan. Your best bet is to slather on that high-SPF sunscreen before you catch some rays.

"Girls, don't make your parents badger you about putting on sunscreen. This is a great way to show us you are becoming more responsible, if you do it yourself without complaining or being reminded! As you show more responsibility, parents will be more comfortable giving you more freedom."

—Julianne, mother of two

Quick Quiz

Tanning is safe for my skin as long as I don't burn. True or False?

What About My Hands and Feet?

You're old enough to know you need to wash your hands thoroughly with soap and water after you go to the bathroom. This helps prevent the spread of germs, which helps you stay healthy. Did you know it takes a while to properly wash off germs? You should wash your hands for as long as it takes you to sing the ABCs to yourself. You should also wash your hands before cooking, eating, or handling food. It's even more important to wash your hands frequently if you or people around you are sick. If you wash your hands a lot, you may need to use a moisturizer after you clean them, especially if they are already chapped and dry.

Nail Care

Germs love to hang out under your nails. Periodically, you should clean under your nails by using one of the sharp nail cleaners that come with fingernail clippers. Clip your nails regularly, too. Use a fingernail clipper and cut them in a slightly curved fashion down to near the end of the white part of the nail. Don't forget your toenails! You'll want to buy separate toenail clippers, which are larger. Toenails should be clipped straight across.

> My mom took me and my best friend for a real manicure for my birthday. It was so much fun! We asked the lady a lot of questions about how to do it ourselves. On the way home, we stopped at the drugstore, and my mom bought us both stuff like a nail file, nail clippers, and nail polish. Now on Fridays, my friend Tina and I do our nails together at home. It's so totally fun!"

Jessica age 11

Preventing and Treating Foot Odor

During preteen and teen years, the sweat glands on your feet start producing more sweat. This can lead to stinky feet. If this is bothering you, there are a few things you can try.

- Clean your feet daily with an antibacterial soap.
- Don't wear the same shoes every day.
- Wear shoes that let your feet "breathe" more, not tight ones that make your feet sweat.
- Sprinkle foot power or baking soda inside your shoes to dry them out when you aren't using them.
- Put a dryer sheet inside your shoes at night to absorb moisture and leave a fresh scent.
- Don't wear socks and shoes all day. Give your feet a chance to breathe.
- If none of this works, try applying a layer of antiperspirant to your feet.

It's a Fact!

Your foot contains 26 bones; 33 joints; more than 100 tendons, muscles, and ligaments; and 250,000 sweat glands!

Q & A with Dr. H

Read the Q & A with Dr. H below. What other questions do you have about skin care? Write them down in your journal. If you don't find the answers to your questions in this book, be sure to talk to your parents or a doctor about them.

Q: *Is it ever okay to pop pimples?*

A: This is so tempting to do, but it is not a good idea. When you do this, you can introduce more bacteria and drive the infection deeper into the skin. It also makes it more likely that your pimples will leave scars. Apply a little spot treatment to the pimple and try not to touch it—it will go away soon!

Q: *I've heard that chocolate causes acne. Is that right? Do any foods cause acne?*

A: No specific foods have been proven to cause acne. Drinking plenty of water might help reduce acne, and an overall healthier diet may have a positive impact on acne. It certainly can't hurt!

Q: *I want to start wearing makeup, but my mom won't let me. How can I convince her?*

A: That's a tough one. Many parents think preteens and young teens are too young to wear makeup. Have an honest talk with your mom. Ask her respectfully about her concerns. Your mom wants to protect you and keep you safe, which includes not letting you grow up too soon! Your mom may not want you to worry about your appearance so much, or she might be concerned about how you are presenting yourself to others. Listen carefully and respond with your own thoughts and feelings. You might be able to find a compromise.

8 Preventing Body Odor

Let's answer your questions...

- **How Do I Prevent Body Odor?**
- **What are Deodorants and Antiperspirants?**

How Do I Prevent Body Odor?

It is pretty simple to keep body odor under control. To reduce body odor, shower once every day and right after exercising. Use a good soap that doesn't irritate your skin. There are a lot of different soap and body wash products out there. Here is some additional advice:

- Just like acne on your face, if you have acne on your body, you can treat it with a soap that has salicylic acid or benzoyl peroxide.
- Take special care to use soap under your armpits. Work up a nice lather, and use a washcloth.
- Change into clean, fresh clothes, socks, and underwear every day and after intense exercise.
- Pick clothes that will breathe well and allow some of your sweat to evaporate.
- If for some reason you can't shower after exercise, try to at least wash under your armpits with a wet washcloth (or use a paper towel if you don't have a washcloth handy).

Quick Quiz

There is nothing you can do to prevent body odor. True or False?

What Are Deodorants and Antiperspirants?

In addition to staying clean, you will probably want to use a **deodorant** or an **antiperspirant**. Deodorants have components that cover up body odor with a scent of their own. They may also contain ingredients that help inhibit the growth of bacteria, which decreases odor. Antiperspirants have a substance in them (aluminum) that actually decreases the amount of sweat that is released onto the skin. You can also buy a combination antiperspirant and deodorant.

There are many varieties and brands of these products available, so finding the kind you like the best may require some experimenting. You can also ask your friends who use them or ask your family members to see what they like and what works for them. Sticks, gels, and roll-on liquids are the most common forms of these products, but you can also get them in sprays, creams, and powders. See what feels most comfortable to you. You can try a variety of scents or try one that's unscented. Use it after you shower, or if you don't shower in the morning, apply it in the morning before you get dressed.

Just For Fun!

Plan Ahead

Take an outing with a parent or friend to the deodorant and antiperspirant aisle at your local drugstore. Choose one or two products you'd like to try, so you'll be ready when you need them.

9 Hair Care

Let's talk about hair care...

- **How Do I Keep My Hair Looking Its Best?**
- **What Do I Do About Body Hair?**

How Do I Keep My Hair Looking Its Best?

Caring for your hair now may be a little different from when you were younger. Because of all the amazing changes happening to you during puberty, your hair might change, too. You may also be taking over responsibility for your own hair care and be making more of your own decisions about your hair. Or you simply might want a new look to go with the new and growing you!

General Hair Care Suggestions

The specifics of your hair care routine will vary according to your hair type and how you want your hair to look. Here are a few general hair care suggestions.

Do:

- Wash your hair regularly. Some girls may need or want to wash their hair every day. Keep in mind that washing your hair removes the natural oils, which actually help keep your hair shiny and healthy. At the same time, you probably don't want your hair to look like it is too oily. Find the balance that works for you!

- Take care of your hair care tools. Periodically wash your brushes and combs in hot, soapy water and rinse them well afterward.

- Brush or comb your hair regularly. This distributes the natural oils in your hair and also keeps your hair tangle free and looking pretty.

- Find the right shampoo for your hair. Try out a few brands to see what works best for your hair.

- Use a conditioner to help manage tangles. If you have oily hair, be sure to keep the conditioner on the tips of your hair. If you have tangles in your hair, work on them gently from the end to the root with a wide-toothed comb. You can do this before you shower or while the conditioner is in your hair in the shower. Make sure the tangles are all combed out before you rinse out the conditioner.

- Be gentle with your hair, especially when it's wet. Wet hair is more easily damaged and broken.

- You might notice white flakes, called "dandruff," on your scalp. These flakes are actually dead skin cells caused by an inflammatory skin condition. Dandruff is common if your scalp is very oily. Often it can be treated with over-the-counter dandruff shampoos. Be sure to talk to your doctor if this doesn't help clear it up.

- Get your hair trimmed about every 8 to 12 weeks. This will help prevent damage to the ends of your hair, called "split ends." Even if you are trying to grow out your hair, an occasional trim will keep your hair looking its best while it grows!

continued on following page

continued from previous page

- Think carefully before you drastically alter your natural hair by using relaxers, perms, or hair coloring. Some of these techniques may damage your hair. Some people are also sensitive to the chemicals used in these products. If you are set on using one of these techniques, get it done professionally and talk to your parents about it first.

- Eat right. Good nutrition is essential for healthy, shiny hair.

> "My hair got so oily I had to wash it every day. But I also noticed it was really shiny, and thicker, too. It took a while to stop wishing it was like it used to be, but when everyone kept telling me how pretty and shiny it was, I liked it better!"
>
> Kerry age 12

Quick Quiz

Dandruff is most common when you have a very dry scalp.
True or False?

- Share your hairbrush or other hair care tools with someone else. Certain infections can be shared this way. There is also a danger of getting head lice, which is a common but treatable problem.
- Overdry your hair with heating products. Hairdryers, curling irons, and other heating products dry out and damage your hair over time. Try to limit the use of these products, or use the coolest setting.
- Forget to wash your hair with shampoo right after swimming in a pool. If you swim often, you may want to use a special swimmer's shampoo.
- Be taken in by the need for endless hair products. Remember, advertisers want you to buy as many products as possible.
- Worry about your hair too much. It's only hair. If you get a haircut you don't like, you can always try again after it grows out.

What Do I Do About Body Hair?

It is common for many girls who live in the United States to want to remove some of the new body hair on their legs, armpits, or other areas. There is no medical reason you have to get rid of new body hair—the reasons are cultural and cosmetic. You might feel self-conscious about your new body hair, even though it's a normal part of your development. Some girls feel a lot of social pressure to remove new hair. You will have to figure out what feels right for you. Be sure to talk to your parents before you start any kind of hair-removal process.

Shaving

Shaving is the most common method for removing body hair. It's inexpensive and relatively easy to learn. It's also pretty safe, even though it's easy to nick your skin when you are learning. On the downside, you have to do it every couple of days if you want your skin to stay really smooth.

If you've decided you are going to shave your unwanted body hair, the best way to learn is to have someone, like your mom or older sister, show you how. Here are some tips to help you:

- First, wet the hair and apply shaving cream. This will soften the hair and make it less likely that you'll cut yourself. Let the hair soften for a few minutes before you start shaving.
- Shave lightly. If you have a sharp razor, you won't need a lot of pressure, and a sharp blade will minimize red bumps afterward.
- Make sure your razorblades are clean and sharp. Frequently change your blades or use a new razor.
- Never borrow a razor. Sharing razors increases your risk of getting an infection.
- After you shave, rinse with cool water and pat dry. You can apply some moisturizer to the area as well.
- Shave against the direction of hair growth for the closest shave, but shave in the direction of hair growth if you want to minimize bumps and razor burn.

Razor Burn and Razor Bumps

Following these good techniques while shaving will help decrease your chance of getting **razor burn** and **razor bumps**. Razor burn is an irritating rash that appears a few minutes after shaving. This is usually caused by not enough lubrication. Try applying less pressure, using fresh blades, using plenty of shaving cream and moisturizer, and shaving in the direction of hair growth.

Razor bumps are a kind of persistent irritation caused by shaving. These bumps are painful and can look almost like acne. Razor bumps are especially a problem for girls who have tightly curling hair. The cut hair actually curls back into the skin, causing the irritation. If you are prone to razor bumps, you can buy special razors and aftershave products that can help, but ask your doctor if you are still having problems. You may need to stop shaving for a while.

It's a Fact!

You might have heard that shaving makes hair grow in darker and thicker. This isn't true. Because hair stubble is thicker, hair may appear to be a bit thicker, but it isn't.

Other Hair Removal Methods

There are several other hair removal methods, but be sure to check with a parent before trying them.

- Tweezers. You can pluck your hairs out one by one by the root with a set of tweezers. This can be painful, and it is only practical if you have a few stray hairs. It would take too long and be too painful to pluck all the hair off your legs!

- Waxing. This involves applying a layer of hot wax to the area where you want to remove hair, and then using a special paper strip to rip out the hairs caught in the wax. This hurts, but some women like it because the waxed areas stay smooth for weeks.

- Chemical creams. Creams with harsh chemicals can be used to dissolve hair.

Also, remember that you don't *have* to remove extra hair.

Plan a Hairstyle Party

Invite your friends over and have them each bring their own hairbrush, comb, bobby pins, clips, and hair ribbons (or you can provide them if you want to, but be sure everyone has their own set). Spread out some fashion magazines and have everyone look for a hairstyle they want to try. Then pair up and help each other create the style. Give prizes for the best hairstyle, the silliest hair style, and so on. Don't forget to take photos!

10 Your Period: What to Do About It

Let's talk about dealing with your period....

- I Got My Period—Now What Do I Do?
- What If I Get My Period When I'm Not Expecting It?
- What Type of Premenstrual Changes Can I Expect?

I Got My Period—Now What Do I Do?

You have different options for dealing with your menstrual flow during your period. Menstrual pads are the most common choice for girls when they first start their period.

Using Menstrual Pads

Menstrual pads (also known as "sanitary napkins") are made from absorbent materials designed to soak up the blood that flows from your uterus during your period. Most menstrual pads have a sticky strip on the bottom. You simply peel off the paper covering the sticky strip and press the pad, sticky side down, to the middle of your underpants. This extra material may feel a little funny at first, but you'll get used to it. Don't worry—nobody will be able to see your pad! Some tight clothing might make your pad noticeable, though, so you might want to check in a mirror if you aren't sure.

You'll need to check your pad at least every few hours and replace it with a new one. Don't go more than four hours without checking and changing your pad. Even if your pad is not full, after a few hours you will probably want to replace it. After several hours, a pad may start to develop an unpleasant odor. (Fresh menstrual flow doesn't have much of an odor.)

When replacing your pad, wrap the old pad in the wrapper of the replacement pad or in a piece of tissue, and put it in the trash. If you are in a public restroom, there is usually a silver box affixed to the bathroom stall just for this purpose. Never put a menstrual pad down the toilet—it will clog the plumbing.

> **I was really shy about telling my mom, and even my friends, when I got my first period. I snuck some of my sister's pads and used those, but they were so uncomfortable. After the second day, I told my mom, and she took me right away to the drugstore. We bought six kinds of pads so I could see what I liked. I wish I'd just told her in the first place. My advice is to try pads before you even get your period, and then you will be prepared and comfortable!"**
>
> *Ellie* age 13

Types of Menstrual Pads

You may have to try a few different types of pads before finding the ones you like best. You can also use different types of pads under different circumstances. For example, you can use a thicker, more absorbent pad the first day or two of your period when the flow is heaviest. You can use thinner pads or panty liners when your flow is lighter.

Tampons

Most girls start out using menstrual pads instead of tampons, but there's no reason you can't start to use tampons even when you have your very first period. If you're planning on going swimming and you get your period, tampons are the best choice. A tampon is a tightly rolled cylinder of absorbent material with a string attached. Most tampons are made of cotton, rayon, or a blend of the two. There are also tampons made from organic cotton. Many doctors recommend that you don't use scented tampons because they are more likely to cause irritation.

Tips for Using a Tampon

- Understand your anatomy! The vaginal canal goes back and up at an angle. You will need to push the tampon far enough into the vaginal canal for it to be comfortable (so you don't actually feel it). The tampon will feel uncomfortable and won't work as well if it isn't fully inserted up into the vaginal canal.

- Pick the right size tampon. It's usually best to start with a small, or "slender," tampon.

- Read the instructions on the package carefully.

- Wash your hands before inserting the tampon.

- Relax. Being tense can make the tampon harder to insert. If you are tense, take big breaths to relax and try again. Or try another time when you feel more patient and calm. It's no big deal! You'll get the hang of it eventually!

- Do not force the tampon if it feels painful. It should not hurt! Try again some other time. If it's still painful when you try to insert a tampon, double-check your angle of insertion.

- You do not have to change your tampon when you urinate—just hold the string out of the way.

- When you aren't swimming, it's a good idea to use a panty liner to soak up any extra flow. This can happen if the tampon gets full.

- Change your tampon every four to six hours. You can keep it in up to eight hours if you need to, and if you aren't leaking. It's important not to leave it in for more than eight hours. If your flow is heavy, you may need to change your tampon more frequently or try a more absorbent tampon.

- Gently pull on the tampon string when you want to remove the tampon. If it is dry or sticks a bit when you pull it, you may want to remove it a little later.

The tampon is inserted into the vaginal opening, and the end with the string hangs out. If the tampon is inserted far enough into the vaginal opening, you can't feel it. There is no danger of the tampon getting "lost" or "stuck" inside you, and if it's inserted correctly, there is no danger of it falling out.

> **The first time I used a tampon, it took a bunch of tries to get it right. I wanted to give up, but I had a pool party to go to and my mom wouldn't let me quit! I'm glad I kept trying because the party was really fun and the tampons worked great!"**
>
> Isabella age 12

Dr. H says: "You can always use a menstrual pad if it is too challenging right now to insert a tampon. Also, you should know that it isn't possible to put the tampon in the wrong opening accidentally—it wouldn't fit inside your urinary opening."

Tampon Safety

If you read the package insert that comes with tampons, you will notice a warning about something called "toxic shock syndrome." Toxic shock syndrome is a serious medical condition that can occur when too many of certain bacteria grow in the vagina. These bacteria love to grow on used tampons that have been in into the vagina for too long. You shouldn't have to worry about toxic shock syndrome if change your tampons regularly. This is why it's important to remove the tampon after a maximum of eight hours and why it's a good idea to use a pad overnight.

What If I Get My Period When I'm Not Expecting It?

This happens to plenty of girls (and women), so don't worry! Here are a few helpful hints about what you can do if this happens to you:

- When you first start menstruating, you will probably stain your underwear at least a few times. This is nothing to worry about. Just rinse them out and put them in the wash when you can.

- Most of the time, when you get your period you will notice a sort of wet feeling. If you have fresh underwear available, you can put those on and then put on a menstrual pad or insert a tampon. If you don't have fresh underwear, just apply the pad to your stained underwear or insert a tampon for the moment until you can get fresh underwear.

- If there are no menstrual pads or tampons around and you don't have a way to get them, you can use several layers of paper towels or toilet paper.

- If you're completely unprepared and you don't notice your period right away, you may stain through to the pants, shorts, or skirt you're wearing. Don't panic! Go to the restroom and try to get the stain out. Or tie a sweater or jacket around your waist until you can get clean clothes.

- Ask for help. Any woman or girl who has her period will understand your predicament and will want to help!

As you get older, your period will get more regular. Some women and girls notice certain changes in the first few days before menstruation, like breast tenderness. After a while, you will get a sense of when you are likely to start menstruating. You can wear a panty liner on those days to catch the beginning of your menstrual flow.

Things you might experience before or during your period:

- Breast tenderness
- Slight puffiness of the skin
- Increased or more severe acne
- Mood changes (like irritability or sadness)
- Food cravings
- Cramps
- Changes in energy
- More thoughtful or reflective feelings

What Type of Premenstrual Changes Can I Expect?

While it is true that some girls have symptoms associated with **premenstrual syndrome**, or **PMS**, for many girls, the symptoms are easy to manage, and some girls have no problems at all.

If you do have some symptoms, there are many things you can do to lessen or eliminate them:

- Eat a healthy diet.
- Avoid caffeine (found in some sodas and coffee).
- Get regular exercise.
- Reduce stress.
- Get enough sleep.
- Reduce your sugar intake.

Dr. H says: "I think our attitude about our own menstrual cycle matters a great deal. In many cultures, a woman's period is seen a special time of reflection and insight, and a woman having her period is seen as a source of wisdom. Many of us do feel more sensitive and introspective leading up to and during our periods. Maybe, instead of getting down on yourself for feeling moody, you can come to appreciate your heightened emotions during this time."

Cramps

You may experience menstrual cramps a day or two before your menstrual flow begins, but they are more common after your flow starts. You might feel them in your lower belly or lower back. The feeling might be a sharp pain or more like a dull ache. Some girls notice them for only a few hours, but others have cramps for longer. Not everyone gets cramps, but here are some things to try if you get cramps:

- Talk to your parents about taking an over-the-counter medication, such as ibuprofen or naproxen. Acetaminophen will also work for milder cramps. Make sure you read all the instructions carefully, and don't take more than the instructed dose.
- Try a heating pad or a warm bath.
- Gently stretch your back and belly.
- Try gentle exercise like walking or yoga.
- Take things a little easier.

Quick Quiz

Every girl gets cramps before and during her period. True or False?

Just For Fun!

Celebrating Your Menstrual Cycle

Many cultures have some sort of celebration when a girl has her first period. I think getting your first period is an exciting and important time in your life. It is a signal that you are growing into a woman! It is a great opportunity to celebrate who you are and who you are becoming. Take some time to think about how you might like to celebrate this amazing event. (You can do this with others or by yourself. It's up to you.) Here are some ideas:

- Go on an outing to someplace you love (a museum, a restaurant, the park, the ocean, or a favorite shop) with friends or a special person in your life, like your mom or grandmother.

- Have a party with your friends and plan some activities that you really enjoy.

- Get some balloons and a cake and have a simple celebration after your family dinner.

- Write a special letter to yourself in your journal. You can write about your hopes and dreams and all the special things that make you who you are!

- Make yourself a special item, like a jewelry box, a beaded necklace, or a picture frame.

- Ask your mom or dad to make your favorite meal for dinner, or make your favorite recipe yourself (like cookies, lasagna, soup, or fresh bread), and share it with your family or friends.

11 Exercise

Let's discuss exercise needs...

- **What Are the Benefits of Exercise?**
- **Is It Possible to Exercise Too Much?**

What Are the Benefits of Exercise?

You've probably heard a lot about how good exercise is for your health today and in the future. This is absolutely true! It's good to get in the habit of exercising now, when you are young. You can take the good habits you establish now with you into adulthood.

Here are some of the ways exercise is good for your health:

- It lowers your resting heart rate, a sign that your heart is pumping more effectively.
- It helps prevent a number of health conditions like heart disease, diabetes, and arthritis.
- It burns calories, which is important for maintaining a healthy weight. When you combine healthy eating with daily exercise, you come up with an amazingly healthy you!
- It helps you deal more easily with the physical challenges of life because it helps build endurance and muscle mass.
- It boosts your energy levels, even when you aren't exercising.
- It can improve your mood and the quality of your sleep.

- It can be a great way to socialize if you exercise with others. Playing a team sport teaches other important skills, like the value of good sportsmanship and teamwork.

- It can help you feel more confident. This can be true if you practice long enough to get skilled at a particular activity, but also when you are just trying out a new activity. You become more confident when you prove to yourself that you aren't afraid to try new things!

Dr. H says: "Exercise is really anything that gets your body moving! It doesn't have to be a sport."

It's great that exercise benefits your health in so many ways, but exercise is also fun! If you don't think exercise is fun, it's probably because you haven't found the right kind of exercise for you.

The trick to enjoying exercise and sticking with it is to find one or more activities that you enjoy. Then it will be easy to establish positive exercise habits. Try to exercise at least a little bit every day.

"After I get home from school, I like to go to my room and dance around to my favorite music. I shut the door so I can be alone and just have fun with no one watching!"

Jill   age 13

Exercise Types

It's a good idea to try different types of exercise:

- **Cardiovascular activities (cardio).** Any exercise that raises your heart rate (like running, swimming, dancing, or biking) is considered a cardio activity. It gets the blood pumping through your body and increases your heart rate. This strengthens your heart and keeps you healthy.

- **Strength training.** This includes any type of exercise that exposes muscles to more weight than is typical. This strengthens your muscles over time. For example, you can do sit-ups to strengthen the muscles in your midsection, you can lift small weights, or you can do push-ups to strengthen your arms and shoulders. You should never try to lift very heavy weights—this can put too much strain on your developing muscles. If you want to try some strength training exercises, have a knowledgeable adult show you how.

- **Stretching.** Stretching your muscles is important when you exercise. Keeping your muscles loose and your body flexible helps prevent injuries. Yoga is one of the best types of exercise for stretching your muscles and learning a variety of ways to stay flexible. You can also do stretches as part of your warm-up or cool-down when you play sports or do other forms of exercise. Stretching also

Quick Quiz

Gardening and walking don't count as exercise. True or False?

relaxes your nervous system, so it is a great way to stay calm and focused.

Exercise Safety

- Warm up with lighter exercise before you start more intense exercise. When you're done with more intense exercise, cool down with some stretching and moving at a slower pace. Try to warm up and cool down for at least five minutes each.

- If exercise is painful, stop and take a break. You shouldn't feel dizziness, chest pain, wheezing, or cramps when you exercise. It's good to challenge yourself, but you shouldn't make yourself feel bad.

- Use the right safety equipment for your activity. Learn about what equipment you need for your activity, and then use it.

- Everybody can exercise in some way. But if you have a major medical problem, or you plan to significantly increase your exercise level, talk with your doctor first.

- Make sure you have the right shoes and clothing. Replace worn-out shoes. Loose cotton or other fabrics that absorb sweat are good choices for exercise clothing. A sports bra is recommended if you have larger breasts.

- If you are injured, follow the advice of your doctor and coach. You can reinjure yourself if you start exercising again too soon.

- Drink enough water, especially if it is very hot when you are exercising.

Is It Possible to Exercise Too Much?

Overexercising is not good for you or your body. If you are participating in a sport, you shouldn't practice that sport more than five days a week. If you are practicing more than that, if you find you are frequently injured or sore, or if your muscles feel tired, you may be overdoing it. Talk to your parents or your coach if you are concerned about this.

Sometimes girls exercise too much because they are trying to lose weight needlessly or in an unhealthy way.

Sometimes this type of exercise is all a girl will think about most of her day. Some girls need medical attention if their relationship with exercise becomes unhealthy.

Do You Like to Exercise?

If you like to exercise, think about how you might share that enjoyment with someone else. Plan a hike with your family, or teach a friend some tips on a sport you like. If you don't like to exercise, think about why you don't. Would it be more fun with friends? Is there any kind of exercise you've always wanted to try? See if you can find a way to try it. Make notes in your journal about your exercise plan, and spend a few weeks keeping track of what exercise you do. It is fun to look back and see what a great job you are doing!

12 Nutrition

Let's talk about nutrition...

- **What Should I Eat to Stay Healthy?**
- **Dr. H's Guidelines for Healthy Eating**

What Should I Eat to Stay Healthy?

You probably have more of a say about what you eat now than you did when you were younger. With the freedom to choose what you eat comes greater responsibility. Your food choices provide a foundation for your health. The saying "you are what you eat" is correct. The food you eat is used to build, repair, and run your body. You need to give your body high-quality fuel.

I've created a few simple guidelines for you when it comes to nutrition. If you follow these rules, you will be on your way to giving your body everything it needs to stay healthy!

Dr. H says: "A nutritious diet helps you maintain a healthy weight, gives you energy to perform all your daily activities, and provides your body with the vitamins and minerals it needs to stay healthy."

Dr. H's Guidelines for Healthy Eating

1. Eat a balanced diet.

In other words, eat lots of different kinds of foods! This will help provide a range of **nutrients**, the chemical substances your body needs to survive and thrive. Each of these nutrients plays a different role in your body. Some nutrients you may have heard of are **carbohydrates** (which are in grains like rice or wheat bread), **fats** (like in olive oil or butter), **proteins** (like in meats, nuts, and beans), and **vitamins and minerals** (especially plentiful in fruits and vegetables). You need to eat a variety of foods to get all of the nutrients your body needs to be healthy. Eating too much of any one food at the expense of the others will make your body out of balance.

Go to www.ChooseMyPlate.gov to get an idea of how to structure your food choices to stay healthy. You'll notice there are big portion sizes for fruits and vegetables. The grain section provides most of the carbohydrates you need. The protein section provides your protein needs. The dairy section provides protein, carbohydrates, and some important vitamins and minerals.

Everyday Foods	Occasional Foods
Baked potato	French fries
Yogurt with fresh fruit	Cherry pie or cake
Apple	Danish with apple filling
Whole grain bread with cheese or peanut butter	Crackers with processed cheese spread
Carrot sticks	Potato chips
Low fat milk	Soda
Bran muffin	Doughnut
Whole grain pancakes	Sugary cereal

Because most people get enough fat in the foods they eat, fat is not shown as a separate category.

2. Know the difference between everyday foods and occasional foods.

Some foods you could eat almost every day as part of a healthy diet. Other foods are better for special occasions. This does not mean a particular food is "bad" or "good." Below is a chart with some examples of everyday foods and occasional foods.

Here are a few more tips about everyday foods versus occasional foods:

- In general, foods that are very high in both sugar and fat (like most desserts) are occasional foods. Foods that are closer to their natural state are more nutritious than more heavily processed foods.

- Try to cut back on foods that have calories but no vitamins or minerals, such as soda.

3. When you are hungry, EAT!

Enjoy your food! You may find yourself hungrier than you used to be, especially as you are going through your growth spurt. You are going to need to take in more calories to support your extra height and weight. If you exercise a lot, you will need to eat to replenish the energy you use. Your brain needs good nutrition to go through all these changes, too. There's no need to count calories. Just listen to your body and respond to your hunger by choosing healthy everyday and occasional foods you enjoy.

4. Don't eat unless you are hungry.

Do you ever eat when you are bored? Do you ever eat in front of the television without even noticing or enjoying it? Do you ever eat because you are feeling a little sad or maybe even angry? A lot of people do this once in a while, but these are not good eating habits, and they can lead to unneeded weight gain. Here are some tips to help you pay attention to your hunger and notice when you are full:

- **Eat slowly.** Take your time eating. Chew slowly and pay attention to how delicious your food is. It takes your brain about 20 to 30 minutes to register that you are full, so give your body a chance to tell you that it's had enough.

- **Notice when you are full.** If you eat slowly, and at a table with your family or friends, it is easier to notice this than if you eat in front of a computer or television. Sometimes food just tastes so good we want to eat more of it even when we are full. If this happens to you, try to remember to stop eating. Remind yourself you can have another serving tomorrow.

- **Don't overstuff yourself.** Eating too much feels unpleasant. Start with reasonable serving sizes. A serving size for a piece of meat is about the size of a deck of cards. The serving size for carbohydrates (like rice or mashed potatoes) is about the size of your closed fist. A serving of fruits and vegetables is also about the size of your fist, but you can usually eat fruits and vegetables without having to worry a lot about serving size.

- **Don't eat to feel good if you are upset.** Sometimes people eat when they are upset about something. They use food to distract themselves from their feelings. This is not a good habit. If you are upset or sad or concerned about something, the best thing to do is to talk to your parents or a trusted adult or friend.

5. Have fun with food.

Food (along with clothing and shelter) is one of the necessities of life. We are so lucky that we need food to survive because food is delicious and can it be fun, too. Try eating new foods and preparing foods in new ways. This is the only way to expand your food choices and find some new favorites.

6. Carry healthy snacks with you.

When you are growing, it can seem like you are hungry almost all the time! Take the time to prepare healthy snacks that you can have with you when you need them. This can prevent you from eating junk food since it won't be the only thing available.

> "The best thing I ever did was keep some healthy granola bars in my locker at school. Sometimes I got so hungry I could eat anything. But now I know I have something good, so I don't eat candy instead."
>
> Jasmine age 13

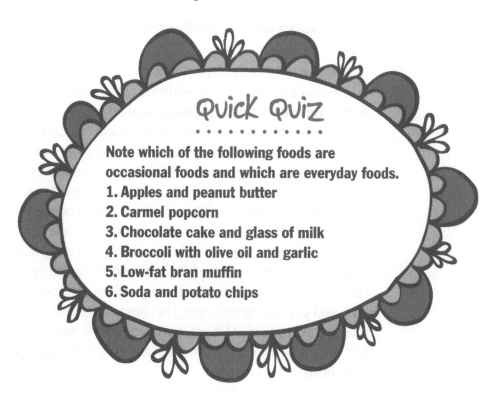

Quick Quiz

Note which of the following foods are occasional foods and which are everyday foods.
1. Apples and peanut butter
2. Carmel popcorn
3. Chocolate cake and glass of milk
4. Broccoli with olive oil and garlic
5. Low-fat bran muffin
6. Soda and potato chips

Healthy Snack Ideas

- Carrot and celery sticks with peanut butter or soy butter
- Low-fat microwave popcorn or packaged popcorn
- Trail mix (ingredients: one-quarter cup whole-grain cereal, raisins or dried cranberries, two tablespoons of sunflower seeds or chopped nuts (consider soy nuts), and chocolate chips)
- Low-fat plain or chocolate milk and whole-wheat pretzels
- Whole-grain crackers and string cheese
- Whole fruit (like apples, pears, or bananas) with string cheese or peanut butter, soy butter, or sunflower seed butter
- Mini-bagel with low-fat cream cheese
- Whole-wheat pretzels and turkey slices
- Baked whole-grain chips and salsa or bean dip

7. Maintain a positive relationship with food.

Food is essential to a happy, healthy life! Sometimes girls develop an unhealthy obsession with their food by eating too much or not enough. In extreme cases, this can lead to **eating disorders** that require medical attention. Doctors rarely recommend a "diet" for preteens and teens. If you are unhappy with your weight, there are steps you can take to change it. Your doctor will likely suggest modifying your diet and exercising a little more, but you still need to eat lot of calories to be healthy. "Fad" diets and skipping meals can actually be dangerous. Never skip meals or try "dieting."

To be healthy and maintain a healthy body weight, you can choose fewer "occasional" foods and more "everyday" foods, only eat when you are hungry, watch your portion size, and get regular exercise. The most important thing is to love the skin you're in! If you think you might have a problem with food, make sure you talk about it with your doctor or another adult you trust.

Caffeine

Caffeine is a substance found in coffee, tea, chocolate, hot chocolate, and many carbonated beverages like cola. Caffeine makes your body feel like it has extra energy. You should limit your use of caffeine to no more than one beverage a day. Too much can make you feel jittery or nervous. In very high doses, caffeine is unsafe for everybody, and even low doses can cause problems for those sensitive to it. If you feel jittery or are having trouble sleeping, cut back on your caffeine or eliminate it completely. Avoid energy drinks and other similar products completely. They have very high doses of caffeine, which can be dangerous.

Just For Fun!

Track What You Eat

Pick a week (seven days in a row) and keep track of what you eat each day in your journal. At the end of the week, look at what you have written with your parents or even with your doctor. This will help you see where you are making good choices and where you might need to make a few changes.

13 Sleep

Let's talk about sleep needs...

- Do My Sleep Needs Change as a Preteen and Teenager?
- How Can I Get Enough Sleep?

Do My Sleep Needs Change as a Preteen and Teenager?

Dr. H says: "Some important hormones, like growth hormone, are released in greater quantities at night. So sleep is super important. Think about all the changes your body is going through during puberty—your body needs to get enough rest to help you grow and change!"

Your sleep needs change when you enter your preteen and teen years. Increased levels of hormones during this time affect the area of the brain that is responsible for setting your inner rhythm. This inner rhythm lets you know when to feel sleepy and when to feel awake. Your brain signals the release of a special hormone involved with sleep. As you get further into your teen years, this hormone is secreted later at night. Because of this, it may become harder to get to sleep early in the evening and wake up early in the morning. This pattern is completely normal, although it can be inconvenient, especially when you have to get up for school.

If you don't get enough sleep, it affects your health. You need enough sleep to be able to concentrate and learn well at school. Students who are sleep deprived can have trouble remembering information. Lack of sleep also can make you moody and less upbeat. In the long term, reduced sleep is associated with a greater risk of certain medical conditions, like diabetes. So it's important to prioritize getting enough sleep.

Sleep Needs

Many different factors affect how much sleep you need. Your age, stage of puberty, stress level, and level of physical activity all play a role. Some people need more sleep than others to function at their best. As a guideline, most preteens and young teens should aim for at least 9 to 10 hours a night. If you wake up in the morning without an alarm clock, you are probably getting enough sleep. If your parents have to drag you out of bed, you probably aren't getting enough sleep.

How Can I Get Enough Sleep?

With homework and perhaps one or more after-school activities, it can be hard to get enough sleep. Going to bed earlier can be challenging, since you may have a harder time falling asleep early than you did when you were younger. But getting enough sleep is a good habit you can develop.

Here are a few tips that may help you get the sleep you need:

- **Try to go to bed around the same time each night, even on weekends.** A lot of preteens and teens go to bed later on weekends. This is understandable, but it makes it even harder to fall asleep when you try to get back in your weekday pattern.

It's a Fact!

Preteens and young teens need at least as much sleep as they did when they were younger and sometimes even more. Your sleep needs will start to decrease when you are an older teen.

- **Make your bedroom a restful place.** You may want to consider studying, watching TV, or using the computer in other rooms of the house. Also, make sure your bedroom is quiet and dark when you go to sleep.

- **Have a bedtime routine.** When you were younger, you probably had a bedtime routine to help get you ready for bed. Now that you are older, you may want to create a new routine. Try to stop using any electronic devices (like your cell phone or computer) at least 30 minutes before bedtime. Instead, make a routine out of taking a shower, reading a book, listening to quiet music, or doing something else that relaxes you.

> **"** I was having a really hard time getting up in the morning, and I was staying up late to do my homework because I didn't get home from basketball and piano until 7:00 p.m. Finally, I decided with my parents that I needed to choose between the two. Now I do basketball during the week and piano only on Saturday. I feel so much better now because I am getting more sleep!"
>
> Jocelyn age 13

- **Assess your activities.** Some young people stay up too late working on homework because their other after-school activities take so much time. Of course, you need to get your homework done. Can you get some of it done earlier in the day? If you can't get to your homework until so late in the evening that you aren't getting enough sleep, you may need to think about whether you are involved in too many activities.

- **Exercise regularly,** but not close to bedtime. Exercise usually makes falling asleep easier, but it can make it harder if you do it just before bed.

- **Avoid eating too much right before bed.** This can make it harder to fall asleep. On the other hand, don't go to bed hungry or your growling stomach might keep you awake!

- **Avoid caffeine in the afternoon or evening.** Cut it out altogether if you can.

- **Is worrying keeping you awake at night?** Emotional upset can definitely make it harder to fall asleep at night. Remember, it is important to deal with your feelings! Try talking to someone you trust, like your parents or a counselor.

- **Sleep in on the weekends if you need to.** If you haven't had enough sleep during the week, you may need to catch up. It doesn't mean you're lazy! But you'll still need to try to get to bed at a reasonable hour.

Keep a Sleep Diary

For one week, keep a diary of your sleep habits. Note the time you go to bed each night and the time you get up each morning. List your bedtime routine, or what you do for the last hour before you go to sleep. Also note how you feel during the day. Are you getting enough sleep? If not, what changes can you to make to get enough?

14 Cigarettes, Alcohol, and Drugs

Let's discuss cigarettes, alcohol, and drugs...

- **What Are the Health Risks of Smoking?**
- **Is Drinking Alcohol Ever Safe?**
- **What Are the Risks of Drugs?**

Dr. H says: "Lung cancer kills more women than any other type of cancer, and this is directly due to tobacco use. Also, heart disease, the number-one killer of women in this country, is greatly worsened by cigarette use. Choosing not to smoke is a big deal for your long-term health!"

What Are the Health Risks of Smoking?

The health risks of smoking are very well documented. You will never have to worry about quitting smoking if you never start smoking in the first place. Smoking increases the risk of multiple kinds of cancer, and it causes heart and lung disease. As people have learned more about the dangers of secondhand smoke, more public places have limited the use of tobacco products.

Many people who smoke started when they were teenagers, which is why you are likely to hear so many antismoking

These are some immediate health risks of smoking:

- It makes your breath, hair, and clothes smell bad.
- It causes shortness of breath, rapid heartbeat, and impaired sports performance.
- It may cause skin to look pale and unhealthy.
- It can cause you to get sick more often.
- It can decrease your general energy level.

Quick Quiz

Smoking causes lung cancer and other cancers, worsens heart disease, and impairs your breathing and sports performance. True or False?

messages now. Fewer girls your age are taking up smoking these days, but far too many still do. The health risks of smoking far outweigh any immediate benefits you might get from it.

Many people seriously underestimate the addictive power of cigarettes. This is why the plan to smoke for a while but quit later is seriously flawed. You may not be able to quit later, or at the very least, it may be a big struggle for you.

Is Drinking Alcohol Ever Safe?

In the United States, it is illegal for people under the age of 21 to drink or purchase alcohol. Still, some teens experiment with alcohol, which includes wine, beer, and liquor. Alcohol is safe in small quantities for most adults, but larger quantities can damage multiple systems of the body. Someone who drinks too much alcohol at once can even die of something called "alcohol poisoning." It is also extremely dangerous and illegal for someone who has been drinking alcohol to drive.

"I already know what to say if someone asks me if I want to smoke or drink or take drugs. I will just say 'NO!' and walk away. Then I will tell my mom. That's my plan."

Suzanne age 11

Quick Quiz

Drinking alcohol is against the law for anyone under the age of 21. True or False?

At some point during your teen years, someone you know might pressure you to try some alcohol. Don't give in to the pressure. Anyone who pressures you to do something you know isn't right is not your friend. Be upfront with your parents if you are ever in this kind of situation.

What Are the Risks of Drugs?

There are many types of illegal drugs, and they have many different effects on the body. Drugs can negatively affect almost every system of the body. Many drugs are highly addictive. That means that over time, a person needs to take the drugs just to feel normal. Drugs have many long-term negative effects, but they can also cause big problems right away.

As with alcohol, at some point, you may be pressured to experiment with illegal drugs. Rely on your best judgment and turn down the offer. If you like, think about some excuse. For example, say, "No thanks, I'm focusing on sports" or "My parents would kill me!" If the person offering you drugs is really your friend, then that should be enough.

Also keep in mind that not all prescription medications are safe. You should never take someone else's medication. Use your own good judgment, but be sure to talk with an adult you trust if a problem arises.

Plan Ahead

Planning ahead is often the best way to be prepared if someone asks you if you want to smoke, drink, or take illegal drugs. It can be easier to make positive choices about drugs if you know what you think ahead of time. Sit down with your parents or another trusted adult, and come up with things you can say if someone offers you any of these substances. What would you say to someone who offered you alcohol or drugs? What if that person was a close friend? Would that change how you felt? Who can you turn to for help or guidance if this happens?

Part Three

Taking Care
of Your Emotions

I n addition to the physical changes that you can see in yourself during this time, there are also changes in yourself that aren't visible. You will spend the next several years growing up, exploring, and discovering who you are as person. It is an exciting time! You will probably start a new school. Some of your interests will change and expand. Relationships with friends and family will change, too. You'll be forming new ideas about who you are and how you fit in the world. This section will help to guide you through these changes.

15 Experiencing Highs and Lows

Let's discuss emotions...

- **Why Am I Experiencing More Mood Swings?**
- **Why Do My Feelings Seem More Intense?**

Why Am I Experiencing More Mood Swings?

During adolescence, hormones such as estrogen go up and down a lot. This can contribute to **mood swings**. Life may seem a little more emotional or dramatic. Issues that used to be small might suddenly seem overwhelming. Everything feels personal. Sometimes you may feel at the top of your game, upbeat and positive, and other times you may feel down in the dumps.

Your feelings may even go up and down in the same day! This variation is a normal part of growing up. Your moods will even out in time. Try to remind yourself that what you are feeling is part of adolescence.

Life Changes

It's not just that your hormones are changing—things in your life like school, sports or other after-school activities, family, and friends are also changing. Even positive change can be stressful. Maybe you have a crush on someone, and you're not sure how this person feels. Maybe you wish your parents would give you more independence, but they aren't sure you are ready for it. Maybe your parents are divorcing, or your family has money problems. Maybe you just won the state spelling bee and are on to the National Championship. Whatever is going on in your life can contribute to your mood.

Give Yourself a Break

It's important not to be hard on yourself when you are going through puberty and experiencing a roller coaster of emotions. The ups and downs you are experiencing are normal. Give yourself a break. Sometimes life and growing up feels stressful, but stress isn't always bad. Everyone experiences stress and has to find ways to deal with it properly. You can learn how to do that, too. Just give yourself time.

> Sometimes I feel super happy, and sometimes I feel really grumpy, and I don't always know why. My doctor said it is totally normal during puberty. She said I should write down my happy times, and when I feel grumpy or sad I can look at them and it might help. But she really wanted me to know that all my feelings are normal and not to worry!"
>
> Helena age 12

Why Do My Feelings Seem More Intense?

You may find yourself feeling your emotions more intensely than before. When you're angry or sad, you're really angry or really sad. This is normal during puberty. Our feelings often give us information about what's important to us and how we would like things to change. Below, we'll talk about some tips for handling a variety of different emotions during puberty and beyond.

- Let yourself cool down a little before you talk with someone who has made you angry.
- Take a few deep breaths and go do something else for a while. This makes it less likely you'll say something unfair or mean, which you might regret later. You can talk to the person who made you angry after you've calmed down.
- When you talk to the person who made you angry, describe what made you angry and how you would like to handle things in the future.
- Remember that name-calling and hurtful comments never make the situation better.
- Listen closely to what the other person has to say, even if you don't agree with it.
- Hopefully you and the other person can come to some sort of understanding, which will make things better the next time the issue comes up.
- Always try to end the conversation on a positive note.

Feeling Angry

It's okay to feel angry. It's important not to stuff away your feelings. But it is equally important to express your anger and use it in appropriate ways.

Feeling Sad

It's normal for all of us to have down days. If something really bad happens, like a grandparent dies, it can take a while to feel better. It is okay to take time to grieve. It's also natural to feel disappointed if you don't get something you wanted, like a part in the school play, or if someone you like doesn't like you in the same way. It's easy to get in a "sorry-for-yourself" mood. That's an okay place to be for a while, but eventually you need to learn how to make yourself feel better.

Consider these ideas the next time you are feeling sad

- **Give yourself a time limit.** Allow yourself to feel really sad for 20 minutes. Set a timer and go ahead and let yourself be blue. When the time is up, move on to something you enjoy doing for at least an hour. If you feel like you want to be sad again, remind yourself that you have to wait until the hour is up. Most of the time, you will forget your sadness and just feel better!

- **Stay busy.** Go for a walk, call a friend, bake cookies, talk to your sister or brother, or play with your dog. Do something to get your mind on what makes you happy.

- **Make lists.** When you are feeling happy, make a list of things you love to do that make you feel good. When you are sad, check the list and do one of those things.

- **Talk to someone.** Talking to a friend or parent is a great way to share your feelings and get support. Talking about what is bothering you (or just talking about the fact that you aren't sure why you feel so sad) is a great way to feel better.

- **Laugh!** Read a joke book, call a funny friend, or watch a silly video or movie. Or just force yourself to laugh at nothing. After a few minutes of laughing, your whole body and mind will feel better!

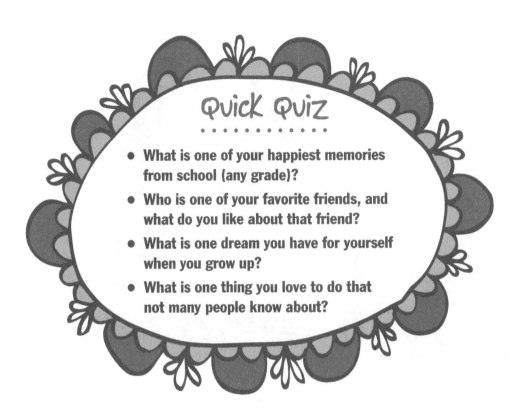

Quick Quiz

- What is one of your happiest memories from school (any grade)?
- Who is one of your favorite friends, and what do you like about that friend?
- What is one dream you have for yourself when you grow up?
- What is one thing you love to do that not many people know about?

Feeling Anxious

Anxiety, or very nervous feelings, can be another challenging emotion to handle. **Stress**, especially stress you are not aware of, can cause anxiety. Things like talking to someone you like, starting a new school, taking a big test, or performing in the school play can also produce nervous feelings. These situations may make your palms sweat and make your heart beat faster. A little anxiety is often a good thing—it gets us primed and ready for action. But anxiety can be a problem if it starts to happen too often, or if it does not seem to go away. If anxiety is keeping you from doing the things you'd like to do, you should talk to your parents and your doctor to find ways to help you feel better and more relaxed.

Feeling Self-Conscious

Almost everyone feels more **self-conscious** while they are going through puberty. There are so many changes happening in your body and in your life that you may feel like everyone is noticing everything about you. Sometimes it might feel as if a spotlight is on you all the time. You may think about your actions over and over. You may worry about how other people will respond to what you say or do. You may feel easily embarrassed, or you may worry too much about how other people feel about you.

While it's normal to be more self-conscious as you go through puberty, you don't want what other people think (or what you think they think) to direct your actions or feelings. Try not to worry too much about what others think of you. As you work on building your self-esteem, you will become less self-conscious.

Dr. H says: "It is important for you to be who you are and do the things you love, no matter what other people might think."

Getting Help if You Need It

Anger, sadness, and anxiety that go beyond normal limits can hold you back and keep you from being the best you can be. Exercising, eating well, sleeping enough, and taking deep breaths can help balance your emotions. However, there may still be times when these emotions are too much to deal with on your own. If you feel like your emotions are overwhelming, you should talk with someone who cares about you (like a parent, your doctor, or another trusted adult). You might also want to ask your parents if you can talk with a professional counselor or therapist. Your school might have a psychologist or social worker you can talk to about how you're feeling—especially if it's getting in the way of your ability to

Dr. H says: "If you feel so bad that you are worried you might hurt yourself in any way, be sure to tell an adult so you can get help right away. You should do the same for a friend you are really worried about."

concentrate and do well at school. Sometimes having a person to talk to who is there just for you is a great way to get yourself feeling back to normal.

Feeling Happy

During puberty, you will also have many awesome, positive feelings and experiences that are special and memorable, like scoring a winning goal, going out with someone special, getting straight A's on a report card, taking a fun trip with your family or friends, having a sleepover, and more! Even your positive feelings will be more intense during adolescence. You will have a lot of happy feelings that you will remember with special fondness as you get older.

Make a Happy List

Write a list of at least 10 things you can do that make you feel happy. For example: Bake cookies, watch your favorite movie, walk your dog, email your best friend a silly joke, call your grandmother, do an art project, read your favorite book, and so on. Once you have a list, keep it handy for the next time you need to boost your mood. Pick one of the things on your list and do it. Then see if you feel better!

16 Self-Esteem

Let's talk about self-esteem...

- How Do I Build My Self-Esteem?
- How Do I Deal with Bullies?

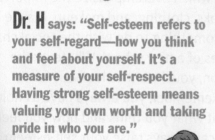

Dr. H says: "Self-esteem refers to your self-regard—how you think and feel about yourself. It's a measure of your self-respect. Having strong self-esteem means valuing your own worth and taking pride in who you are."

How Do I Build My Self-Esteem?

Self-esteem is like the foundation of a house. If it is strong, the house will be sturdy and able to weather storms and strong winds. If the foundation is weak, the house is at risk of falling down or crumbling when the weather gets rough. Your self-esteem is the foundation of you! If you love and respect yourself, then you will have a strong base during the sometimes-rocky path of your preteen and teen years—and throughout your adult life.

Poor Self-Esteem

Having poor self-esteem can make it harder to make good choices for yourself. If you don't respect yourself, it is easier for other people to influence you and your decisions. Some of these people may not have your best interests at heart. Poor self-esteem can make you less confident and less likely to try new things. If you are less confident, it's harder for you to take on new challenges and succeed at them, which can help build self-esteem. When you feel like you aren't worth anything, you often start to treat yourself like that. Other people might begin to treat you that way, too.

> " I remember when my best friend told me she thought I was really bad at science. I believed her. And for the whole school year, I felt bad about myself because I thought she must be right. I even thought I was bad when I got an A on my report card. I finally talked to my mom about it, and she said my friend probably had bad self-esteem about her science grade and was maybe jealous of how good I was. My mom said I should talk to her. I did talk to her. Boy, was I mad! We made up, but I learned a big lesson. Now I don't listen to what other people say about me. I just listen to myself."

Anna age 13

It is common for many girls' self-esteem to dip in early adolescence. Some girls who used to be bold and self-confident start to doubt themselves. It is hard to say why this happens. Maybe girls start to notice some of the messages from the media, which overemphasize the importance of looks, clothing, and makeup. Maybe it has something to do with the social challenges of a new school. Whatever the reason, you'll want to look out for it.

Remember, you always have a choice about what you think and how you feel. You can always raise your self-esteem just by being aware and trying!

Other People and Your Self-Esteem

How much should you let other people's opinions influence your self-esteem? That is a tricky question. On one hand, it builds your self-esteem when someone you respect praises you and shows you that your contributions are valuable. How we feel about ourselves is often mixed with how we think others feel about us. Everyone wants to feel accepted and respected. On the other hand, there are situations when listening to the opinions of others can be damaging and unhelpful. Not everyone's opinion is worth listening to! At the most fundamental level, self-esteem is something you can't get from someone else. You have to give it to yourself.

"Self-esteem is hard to explain to preteens. I think most girls and women struggle with self-esteem at one time or another. The lesson I learned is this: It does not matter what anyone else thinks about you—whether it is good or bad. In life, all that matters is what you think about yourself, and we are all in total control of that. Self-esteem is a journey, and as we travel through life we can continue to improve our self-esteem, even if we are 100 years old!"

—Beth, parent of two

How Do I Deal with Bullies?

Sometimes **bullying** happens without a person even knowing it. You might even have been a bully yourself without meaning to be. Bullying includes physical fights between two or more people, but teasing and name-calling can be forms of bullying, too. Excluding a person from a group can be a form of bullying, as can spreading rumors (things that are not true or that are private or hurtful) about someone. Bullying can happen in person or through text messages, through email, or on the Internet. All of these forms of bullying should be taken seriously. You do not have to put up with bullying as part of growing up. Many states now have laws about bullying, and schools are required to enforce those laws and to educate their students about bullying.

What can you do if everyone is bullying you? Here are some approaches you might try:

- Avoid or ignore the bully. If you have to, get yourself to a safe place.
- Try not to show how upset the bully makes you. This is part of what keeps bullies going. You can talk about it later to an adult.
- Calmly but firmly tell the bully to stop bothering you. This shows the bully you aren't scared, and it can feel good to stand up for yourself.
- Get help from friends. It's harder to pick on someone who has friends around.
- Get help from an adult. Do not hesitate to do this, especially if you've tried other ideas, but they aren't working.
- Never blame yourself for being bullied—it isn't your fault.
- If someone is bullying you online or on a cell phone, get help from an adult. Show the adult the messages or texts before you delete them.

Dr. H says: "Take responsibility for your well-being by being active and getting help if you need it, or use your courage and self-esteem to stand up for yourself."

Look at Yourself

Take a good, hard look at your own behavior. Do you ever bully others? People who bully others often feel insecure about something. If you have bullied someone, think about how you were feeling at the time and how you felt afterward. Counselors and teachers can help you find better ways of dealing with your feelings.

Quick Quiz

- You say mean things to other kids on purpose. True or False?
- You pick fights with kids who seem weak or shy. True or False?
- You write text messages or emails that are hurtful or cruel. True or False?
- You tell lies about other kids. True or False?

If you answered "True" to any of these questions, you may be bullying others. Talk to your parents or a counselor for ideas on why you are treating other kids this way. Get help changing your behavior. You can also make changes on your own by deciding you won't treat others this way anymore!

Who You Are Is Important

Remember, you are totally, one hundred percent unique! There is no one else in the world exactly like you! You are a special individual with talents and gifts that are yours alone. Be proud of your strengths and talents. You have valuable contributions to give the world. Also remember to be grateful for your efforts and your mistakes. Often, you can learn just as much about yourself from your mistakes as from your successes. You can always be proud of trying and failing. We all make mistakes. Meeting the challenge and trying is what matters most!

Just For Fun!

Exercise Your Self-Esteem

- **Make a list of some of the qualities you value in yourself and things that make you feel proud.** Don't be shy! Now is the time to build that strong foundation, so when a storm blows in you can stand strong.
- **Ask friends what they value about you.** Be sure to return the favor and tell them what you appreciate about them!
- **Think about areas where you can improve your self-esteem.** For example, do you feel you don't do well enough in your schoolwork? Do you worry you don't have enough friends? Do you think you should be better at sports? Just because there is something you might like to change about yourself doesn't mean you have less value as a person. Remind yourself of that, and discuss it with an adult you trust. Come up with a plan to improve your self-esteem in each area you'd like to improve. For example, if you want to do better in school, maybe you need to get a tutor in a particular subject, or maybe you can study an extra half hour every night. Make a plan and see how it goes!
- **Try doing something to help someone else.** Not only will this make you and the person you help feel good, but it is also a great way to build self-esteem.

17 School

Let's answer your questions...

- How Do I Manage New School Stresses?
- How Do I Improve in School?

How Do I Manage New School Stresses?

At your age, you probably spend more hours at school than any other place besides your home. School can be a lot of fun, but it can also be stressful. Often, when you reach middle school, your workload increases. Sometimes, the pressure to do well and to get things accomplished also increases. In addition, there are other things to balance, like getting along with new teachers, having a locker, and moving from classroom to classroom throughout the day. You might also be involved in sports, music, drama, or other activities after school. Your life is full and busy! Going to your activities, getting your homework done, and getting to bed on time each day can be a real challenge.

You might be experiencing social changes, too. If you're going to a new school, you may need to make new friends. You may start to expand your friendships and perhaps leave some old friends behind. As we talked about in the previous chapter, you

will be going through a variety of feelings as you find your way through puberty, and this can make social situations more challenging.

Don't forget the excitement and joy in your life! You will begin to accomplish new things, make new friends, and have new and fun experiences as you grow. All of these happy events take energy!

How Do I Improve in School?

No matter how challenging a subject is for you at school, you can always find a way to improve. Here are some tips:

- Keep a positive attitude.
- Let your teacher know that you want to improve.
- Ask you teacher what he or she suggests so you can get help. Often teachers are happy to spend extra time with you before school or during a study hall.
- Ask your guidance counselor for suggestions.
- Talk to your parents. They may be able to find you a tutor in a subject area that's difficult for you. Sometimes high

school or college kids in the area will do this for a very reasonable cost (and sometimes for free).

- Spend extra time going over the subject matter with your mom or dad or even with an older sibling.

Get Organized

Being organized is one the best things you can do to reduce school stress. Here are some helpful ideas:

Dr. H says: "There's almost always something you can do to bring up your grades in a subject, as long as you are willing to work at it. Look at it as a challenge that will improve your self-esteem!"

- Keep a weekly calendar of all your school assignments and after-school activities to help you plan your time each day.

- Use a study calendar to keep track of your assignments and when they are due. Write down everything and cross off assignments as you finish them. Before you go home from school, make sure you have everything you need to complete your assignments.

- Make sure you have an organized way of keeping your assignments, such as a folder for every class.

- At home, have a well-lit, uncluttered, quiet space to use for homework and studying.

- If you have an assignment you are really dreading, promise yourself a little reward when you finish.

- Make sure you start your homework early enough in the evening so you'll be able to finish it without staying up too late.

- Use your organizational skills to make your homework neat and readable.

❝ I was having a really hard time in math, and I didn't want anyone to know. I was even too embarrassed to talk to my teacher. Finally, one day she asked me about it after all the kids had left class. She told me there was someone who could help me out after school. My grades went up after just three weeks of working with a tutor. It feels really good to be getting better at math."

Georgia age 12

Get Help

If you need help, ask for it! Start with yourself! Commit to making your best effort to stay organized and reduce your school stress. Besides your teachers, your parents and older siblings may be a great resource to help with a particular subject. Have them quiz you for tests, and listen to their explanations and suggestions. It may also help if you have a study buddy from your class. Plan a time to work together on assignments and to study for tests. You can quiz each other and help each other learn.

Some students need to be tested for learning disabilities—learning challenges that need extra attention. If you need to learn information in a particular way, it does not mean there is something wrong. It simply means you have a special way of processing certain information and you need assistance to learn how best to do that. Some students learn better from reading, others from listening, and still others by just figuring out things for themselves. There are specialists who can help you understand how you learn best, and they can give you the tools you need to excel in all your schoolwork.

Dr. H says: "Remember, if you are struggling and stressed, it's important to ask for help. There are all kinds of people and resources available for kids to help them do their very best in school!"

Quick Quiz

If I need help in school, I can ask my teacher, my parents, or my guidance counselor for help. True or False?

Get Challenged

You may find that some of your classes are too easy. This may cause you to feel bored and unfocused in class and uninterested in completing assignments. This is a source of stress that you need to address. Here are some ideas for how to handle this:

- **Talk to someone.** Let your teacher or parents know that class is too easy. Sometimes a teacher can give you more challenging books to read or more difficult assignments to complete.

- **Find a tutor.** Tutors who excel in a certain subject can provide more challenging homework and more interesting information than you get in class.

- **Take an advanced class.** Some schools have honors or advanced classes in certain subjects. Ask your teacher or guidance counselor.

- **Look for other opportunities.** Try to find ways to improve your own education and keep it interesting. Go to the library and ask the librarian for suggestions of books to read. Use the Internet to research a chosen topic. There are a lot of fun websites for those who need help or want advanced work!

Focus on Your Strengths

It is important for your self-esteem to focus on your strengths. This is also important for reducing stress. Remember, no one can excel at everything! We all have different strengths and different weaknesses. You may have trouble in English but be a whiz at math. You might be great at track but not at basketball. Praise yourself for whatever you are good at, and ask for help and make a plan for whatever you want to improve in. Also, remember that it's just as important to be a good friend, to have a good sense of humor, and to be willing to help others as it is to be good at schoolwork. Don't forget to focus on those positive qualities!

Just For Fun!

Think About School

Take some time to think about school. What, if anything, is causing you stress? If you feel like everything is going well, write down the things that are helping you. For example: You are organized, you have a tutor, you have helpful friends, and so on. If you are stressed about something, write it down and find a trusted adult to help you make a plan to reduce that stress. For example, if you are struggling in math, ask your mom to help you make a plan to improve.

18 Friends, Cliques, and Peer Pressure

Let's talk about friends, cliques, and peer pressure...

- **How Do I Fit In at School?**
- **How Can I Be a Good Friend?**
- **How Do I Handle Peer Pressure?**

Dr. H says: "If your group of friends excludes other people, is mean to others, or forces you to do things or act in ways that you do not like or that make you uncomfortable, you may need to think about whether this clique is really for you. When you exclude people from your life for no particular reason, you may be missing out on some great friends and some really fun experiences. It is never a good idea to be mean for any reason."

How Do I Fit In at School?

During your preteen and teen years, friendships start to become more important. Your friends and social relationships take on a bigger role in your life as you become more independent from your family. Wanting to fit in with your peers is a normal part of growing up.

Good Cliques

It's common to form deep connections with a small group of people. Such a tightly knit

group is often called a **clique** (pronounced "click"). Cliques are not necessarily bad. Good cliques:

- Include friends who really care about you and whom you feel you can talk to about anything.
- Have people who can count on one another for help and support one another's goals.
- Help make you kind and sociable with a lot of other kids in your class.

Bad Cliques

Unfortunately, there can be negative sides to cliques. People in some cliques encourage one another to be mean or stuck-up. They tell you who you can and cannot hang out with. Some cliques gossip or tease a lot. Others might try to pressure you into doing things you don't really want to do. If you begin to feel uncomfortable or unhappy with your group of friends, you may need to think about whether it is the right group of friends for you. It may be challenging to leave the group, but you should always have the freedom to choose your friends.

Evaluating Your Clique or Group of Friends

If you think you may need some new friends, ask yourself if your clique likes you for who you really are. Are the people in your clique trying to make you become just like them, or do they allow you to be yourself? Do they have rules about what you can wear, what activities you can or can't do, and which people you are allowed to socialize with? Are your friends trying to get you to become someone you aren't?

If the answer to most of those questions is yes, then you may need some different friends. Part of growing up is learning to make hard choices, especially when they are the right choices! You can always ask your parents or another trusted adult for help or advice, too.

Other Relationships

If you choose to be part of a clique, be sure you don't let the clique keep you from exploring other relationships and friendships outside the group. If your friends don't allow you to socialize with anyone outside your group, you will not only miss out on meeting a lot of interesting and fun people but you will also be allowing other people to make decisions for you.

There is no reason you have to be part of a clique to be happy. What will make you happy is having friends who accept you for who you are and who support your interests and goals. A lot of girls have several close friends, but those friends may not all be close with one another. There's nothing wrong with that.

How Can I Be a Good Friend?

Have you ever heard the saying, "The best way to have a good friend is to be a good friend?" It's true! Friendship is definitely a two-way street. Think about how you treat your friends. Are you a good listener? Do you support your friend if she is going through something hard? Do you ever gossip about her or criticize her behind her back? If you treat your friends the way you would like to be treated, you will eventually have some very good and loyal friends!

The Popular Crowd

It is human nature to want to be liked and accepted. This is especially true during your preteen and teenage years. At some point, you may notice there's a "popular" group of kids at school.

There's nothing wrong with being a member of a popular group, and there is nothing wrong with not being a member of this group. Sometimes kids are in this crowd because they are super friendly and well liked by almost everyone. Sometimes kids are in this group for other reasons.

If you are not friends with a popular group of kids, and you really want to be, ask yourself why it is so important to you. It's natural to want to be well liked, but do you want to be friends with a popular group for the right reasons? If being friends with this group does not fit with your interests and values, then maybe it will be better for you not to become a member of this group.

Dr. H says: "Be genuinely friendly and outgoing with all your peers, and you might be surprised by how popular you become just by being yourself!"

When Friendships Fade

At this stage of your life, you and your friends are going through a lot of changes. You are developing new interests and taking on more adult roles, and so are your friends. In the middle of all this, sometimes old friendships fade and come to an end. Sometimes you are the person who needs more distance from your old friend, and other times you are the one who is left behind. This can bring up a lot of challenging feelings, like sadness and maybe even low self-esteem. But fading friendships are normal both now and when you're an adult. It's important to acknowledge your feelings but also to remind yourself that losing a friend does not mean there is something wrong with you or your old friend. However things work out, you can always enjoy the memories of the time you spent as friends in the past. Focus on the friends you have now, and make room for new friendships in your life, too!

How Do I Handle Peer Pressure?

Even adults are influenced by the behavior and approval of their friends and peer group. Sometimes peer pressure is good! Our peers' influence may help us make all sorts of positive changes in our lives. For example, if you make some friends who enjoy biking, you are more likely to start biking with them. Sometimes, though, friends can influence us in less positive ways. This is usually what people are talking about when they refer to **peer pressure**. Peer pressure happens when you feel like you should do something just because your peers think you should, even when you don't want to or when you know it is wrong.

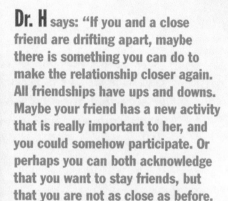

Dr. H says: "If you and a close friend are drifting apart, maybe there is something you can do to make the relationship closer again. All friendships have ups and downs. Maybe your friend has a new activity that is really important to her, and you could somehow participate. Or perhaps you can both acknowledge that you want to stay friends, but that you are not as close as before. Sometimes friends drift apart and then come back after they have explored other interests and other relationships."

Most adults have developed a more solid understanding of who they are, and they have more confidence in what they believe, so they are less likely to be influenced by others in negative ways. This is harder at your age. You are just beginning to figure out what you believe, what you feel is right or wrong, and who you are as a person. That's why your friends' opinions influence you more. Again, this isn't necessarily wrong. It is just important for you to be aware of the ways peers influence you. That way you can decide if they are positive or negative influences.

"One of the reasons parents want to keep track of who their kids' friends are is because of peer pressure. Parents want to be sure that their kids are being influenced by their friends in positive ways. A true friend will respect your decisions and wishes and won't pressure you once you've made yourself clear.""

—Lisa, parent of one

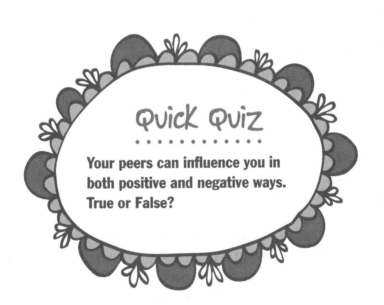

Quick Quiz

Your peers can influence you in both positive and negative ways. True or False?

Make a New Friend

It is wonderful to have a new friend. Maybe someone new moved into your neighborhood or started at your school. Maybe you just started a new activity or joined a new club. Maybe there is someone at school you don't really know, but you would like to get to know that person better. Find your courage, introduce yourself, chat about things you may have in common, eat lunch with this new person, and maybe make a plan to get together after school or on the weekend. Remember, the best way to have a good friend is to be one!

19 Romance and Crushes

Let's talk about romance and crushes...

- Why Do I Like Boys In a Different Way Than I Used To?
- What About Breaking Up?

Why Do I Like Boys In a Different Way Than I Used To?

As part of growing up, your feelings about boys may change. When you were younger, you may have thought of boys as just friends, but as you grow up, there may be a particular boy that you begin to have special feelings toward. These feelings are natural and normal, but they may also be new to you. You may be unsure how to handle them. Part of being a preteen and teenager is learning to understand all your feelings, including romantic ones.

You might also have something called a **crush** on someone. Almost everyone has crushes while growing up. Sometimes the person you have a crush on is someone your age. But a lot of girls get crushes on someone older than them, like an older teen or an adult. You can even have a crush on someone you don't really know, like a movie star or a singer. If you have a crush on someone you know who is your own age, you might want to see if there is a way to spend more time with that person. That way you can find out if you still like that person once you get to know him or her better.

Going Out

You might notice some boys and girls pairing up with each other. Sometimes this means the couple spends time together at school, or they talk on the phone or text each other. Other times this means the couple does things together outside school, either alone or with a group of friends.

> **Dr. H** says: "Sometimes, if you have a crush on somebody, it can be nice to just enjoy the crush. Nobody has to know about it if you don't want them to."

Be sure to talk to your parents to make sure it is okay with them for you to go out with someone special. Some parents might be fine with you spending time with a guy on a group outing, as long as you are supervised by adults. Other parents may not want you to go out with someone you like at all. Be straightforward with your parents about what you want. But be prepared to listen to their thoughts, too. Also remember that if someone does not like you romantically, it does not mean there is something wrong with you. The important thing is to not let it put a big dent in your self-esteem.

Taking It Slowly

If it's okay with your parents, and you do pair up with a boy, remember to take things slowly. Don't get so absorbed with the boy that you forget about your friends, your schoolwork, or your activities. Some couples kiss, but others don't. No one should ever pressure you, and you should never pressure someone else. Trust your instincts and get out of any situation that doesn't feel right.

Some girls aren't ready for this couple stuff at all. That is totally fine, too! There is no reason to rush anything, and there is no right age to become interested in romance. You shouldn't feel pressured into having a boyfriend until you are ready.

Dr. H says: "An important thing to remember as you begin to explore your romantic feelings and crushes is that, like everything in life, there will be ups and downs. Romantic relationships give you the chance to enjoy new people in a new way and learn how to be a good romantic friend and partner. They also teach you about how to handle hurt, and that's important, too. It is all a part of growing up."

Quick Quiz

If you want to go out with someone special, it is important to talk with your parents and find out their guidelines for pairing up and going out.
True or False?

What About Breaking Up?

Sometimes, especially when you're younger, romantic relationships come and go. This might not be a big deal, but it might hurt. It's important to acknowledge disappointed and hurt feelings. But try not to let that be all you think about. Keep busy, hang out with your friends, and do things you enjoy.

If you are breaking up with someone, try to be sensitive about it. Be considerate enough to explain yourself in person. Don't have your friends deliver the message, and don't break up in a text or email. No matter what happens, you will have learned something about yourself, which will help you in future relationships.

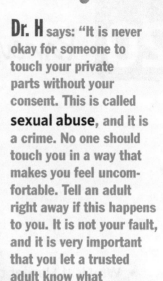

Dr. H says: "It is never okay for someone to touch your private parts without your consent. This is called **sexual abuse**, and it is a crime. No one should touch you in a way that makes you feel uncomfortable. Tell an adult right away if this happens to you. It is not your fault, and it is very important that you let a trusted adult know what happened."

> " My first boyfriend broke up with me in an email. I didn't understand why, and he never really explained. I decided I would never do that to someone else. So when I broke up with my next boyfriend, I told him at lunch. It was hard to do in person, but I think it's better."

Alisha age 13

Just For Fun!

Make a "Crush" Collage

Do you have a crush on someone? What are your thoughts about romance and crushes? Find some old magazines, newspapers, greeting cards, and other materials, like markers and scraps of ribbon. Cut out words, phrases, photos, or sayings that help you express your feelings about romance and crushes. Make a collage in your journal and decorate it with markers, drawings, and your own words.

20 Parents

Let's talk about relationships with your parents...

- **Why Is It Harder to Get Along with My Parents?**
- **Do What Is Expected of You**

Why Is It Harder to Get Along with My Parents?

Whether you are being raised by your parents, grandparents, or other guardians, you are growing up and taking on increasing amounts of responsibility. You are also becoming more independent. At the same time, you are still rooted in your family life. You still depend on your parents for food, material possessions, advice, and attention. As you push for more independence, it's your parents' job to protect and guide you to make sure you are ready for new responsibilities. There's almost certainly going to be a little friction as you and your parents work through this transition. Your parents aren't trying to be unreasonable. They just have a different perspective and a different job to do than you do.

Good Communication with Parents: Some Basics

There are some general principles that can make communication with parents a little easier.

- **Remember to keep your cool.** It's absolutely fine to get upset about something. But when you are very emotional, it isn't usually the most effective time to communicate. Yelling, slamming doors, or name-calling isn't likely to get you what you want. Most likely it will make things worse. Take some time to cool off and then explain what is bothering you. If you are in the middle of a discussion and it starts to get heated, tell your parents you need to take a break. Come back when you are better able to communicate calmly.

- **Listen.** Often your parents have insights that can help you. Try to listen to what they have to say with an open mind, and consider their feelings. Also, if you show your parents you care about their concerns and perspectives (even if you don't agree), they are more likely to negotiate with you and listen to your thoughts, too.

- **After you've listened, explain your own position calmly.** Try to help your parents see the situation from your perspective by using "I" statements. Try to avoid language that is too extreme, like the words "always" and "never." For example, say, "I feel like you don't let me hang out with my friends enough," instead of "You *never* let me hang out with my friends."

- **Act like an adult.** If you can act respectfully toward your parents, they are more likely to see you as capable of handling more responsibility. Accept their final decision gracefully, even if it isn't what you wanted. Remember, as you mature, your parents might have a different perspective on the issue.

- **Pick your battles.** Don't argue over every rule or every decision your parents make. Rather, pick those that are most important to you. If you argue about everything, you will simply make your life (and your parents' lives) miserable. Your parents won't be able to tell what really matters to you. You are more likely to get what you want in a specific instance if you don't fight about every little thing.

- **Be ready to negotiate.** Sometimes you and your parents can come to an agreement that has some of what you want and some of what they want. Be open to compromise. If you make a compromise, make sure you live up to your end of the bargain.

Do What Is Expected of You

In general, parents are more likely to give you more privileges when they see you are ready to handle these privileges. This happens over time when you consistently follow rules and do what you are supposed to do without complaint. If you haven't been doing your homework or chores and you've been rude to your parents all week, it's unlikely your parents are going to let you go to a movie with your friends. Doing what is expected of you helps build your parents' trust. Family rules differ when it comes to chores, curfew, phone privileges, and a lot of other topics. Respecting the rules of the house puts you in a stronger position to negotiate.

" I kept begging for an allowance each week. My mom said that once I showed responsibility around the house, I could get an allowance. I had three chores to do every day: make my bed before school, unload the dishwasher, and take out the trash. Well, I didn't do any of those things every day. Every time I asked for an allowance, my mom just repeated the rules. When I finally got my chores done every day for two weeks straight, I came home from school, and my mom had left me note and $10.00 for the week. The note said, 'Responsibility has its rewards. Great job. Keep it up!' And I do. Because if I don't, I don't get my allowance, and I want to be able to get other privileges, too."

Heather age 11

Let Them In on the Details

Letting your parents in on the details of your life helps build trust as well. When you were a little kid, you probably told your parents everything. Now that you are older, you may want to have more privacy. That is normal! But parents need to know some information about your life. It's reasonable for them to want to know what's going on at school, with friends, and with extracurricular activities; what your mood is; and where you're going and what you'll be doing at a certain time. Giving your parents the information they need to keep you safe and guide you will help you build trust, which will likely result in greater independence.

Keep Asking Parents for Advice

Keep asking for your parents' advice and perspective. Your parents have important life experiences they can share with you. They have made mistakes along the way and learned from them, and they can share what they have learned with you. You will likely learn a lot from your parents if you are willing to listen. Even if you listen to their advice, you will probably still make some mistakes. Everyone makes mistakes. It's part of growing up.

Prove It

Remember, your parents may not always know how best to react to your needs. One minute you may act more like a kid, and the next minute you may act quite grown up. This can make it challenging for parents to know how much independence you are really ready for. Show them you are ready to be more independent by sticking to the rules, listening, and communicating. Prove to them you are becoming more and more responsible. That's the best and easiest way to gain more independence and privileges.

Quick Quiz
. . . .

Good communication with my parents includes taking a break from a discussion if I am getting too upset. It's okay to cool off and come back later to finish the discussion. True or False?

Thinking About Privileges

Is there some privilege you'd like to negotiate with your parents? Think about something that you might want to discuss. First, write a list of all the points you want to make and focus on the positive points. Then, see if you can predict what your parents' concerns will be, and write those down. How can you address those concerns? After you have done this, you are prepared to have a calm discussion. Set a time to talk with your parents. Remember, you might need to compromise. After your discussion, write down the outcome. Did you stay calm? Did you discuss all your points? Is there something you can do better next time?

21 Discovering Who You Are

Let's talk about discovering who you are...

- Who Do I Want to Be?
- How Do I Set Goals for Myself?

Who Do I Want to Be?

It may be hard to understand right now, but the choices you make every day direct your life and shape the person you are becoming. The cool thing about being human is that we can always choose to change. This is a great time

to begin making choices about the kind of person you want to be. It really is up to you! It is a wonderful and sometimes overwhelming idea, but to a large extent, you really get to choose the person you want to be. You don't get to choose your eye color or whether your hair is naturally curly or straight, but you have a lot of control over the attitudes you take and the choices you make.

As you mature, you'll start to form your own opinions about a variety of topics. Instead of just accepting everything your parents say, you may start to look at things from multiple perspectives. You may start to have different ideas about how things should be done. This can lead to some confusion. You'll be learning all sorts of new things about the world, and you may not like everything you see. During this time of your life, it's natural to question long-held beliefs and opinions. Developing your own beliefs and opinions will help you learn more about yourself and what's important to you.

Dr. H says: "Over time, many of your beliefs will become more complex. Right now, you may think of things in clear-cut, black-and-white terms. The truth is that many things in life are very complicated. As you grow, you will begin to see this. You will practice your beliefs, change them, learn from them, and maybe change them again. This is a part of growing up, and it will continue for your entire life!"

Developing Your Own Beliefs

Your preteen and teenage years are a natural time to question your beliefs. Part of becoming an adult involves developing your own belief system. Developing your beliefs takes time. It doesn't happen all at once. You'll build your beliefs piece by piece, and you'll change your mind about some things as you go. You may not know what you think or feel about a lot of things for a while. That's okay! Start by listening to your own thoughts and those of others. Try to be respectful of others' beliefs, even if you disagree with them.

Try Something New

One of the best ways to learn about yourself is by trying something you've never done before. Trying something new builds your self-esteem and helps you realize your strengths! You may end up doing some of the new things you try for the rest of your life. Some things you may try once and never do them again. This is part of exploring the world. So don't be afraid to try new things!

Dig Deeper

This is also a great time to explore interests you already have even further. You are smarter and more mature than you used to be, which makes interests you already have more exciting. For example, if you really love playing the piano, maybe now you can get more serious about it and practice for competitions. If you already love to cook, you could take cooking classes and learn to prepare new foods. If you enjoy running, swimming, or playing a sport, you might consider trying out for a school team or a traveling team. For every activity, there is always a new, richer layer to explore.

If you no longer enjoy an activity you've been doing for a while, try talking to your parents about it. They might support you taking a break from it if they know there's another activity you'd like to try instead.

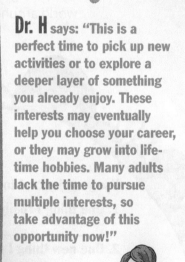

Dr. H says: "This is a perfect time to pick up new activities or to explore a deeper layer of something you already enjoy. These interests may eventually help you choose your career, or they may grow into lifetime hobbies. Many adults lack the time to pursue multiple interests, so take advantage of this opportunity now!"

Your Social Self

Figuring out who you are often happens through your friendships. You might begin to define yourself partly by who your friends are and what you do together. Your friends will start to influence the beliefs you form about the world, and you will influence theirs.

Many of your relationships with your peers will change a lot during these years. You may be friends with a group of girls for a year, but then realize you don't enjoy hanging out with them as much as you used to. This change isn't always easy to deal with, but it is to be expected. You are changing a lot, and your friends are, too. It's best to keep an open mind about yourself and about others in your life. Remember, you aren't defined by any single relationship in your life. Your social self is just part of who you are.

"As you grow and explore your world, remember that what matters most is not accomplishing a goal, but having the courage to try! It is the trying that counts, no matter what the outcome is."

—Nancy, mother of two

Learning About the World

A lot of figuring out who you are involves learning about the world around you. Learning more about the lives, customs,

Quick Quiz

Use your journal to fill in the blanks:

1. One thing I really love to do is
   _____.

2. One new thing I really want to try this month is
   _____.

3. One place I have never visited and really want to see is
   _____.

4. One person I'd like to get to know better is
   _____.

5. If I had to choose right now, I would be
   _____
   when I grow up.

beliefs, and political systems of other cultures and countries will influence how you see yourself in the world. As you learn more about the world, you'll be better able to picture how you'd like to fit into it or how you'd like to change it for the better.

Shaping Your Character

Celebrate the power you have to be the person you want to be! Think about what you want your **character** to be. Do you want to be considerate? Confident? Easygoing? Think about the qualities you most admire in yourself. What are they? For example, do you love being helpful to everyone, even strangers? Maybe you want to develop this quality by volunteering in a food pantry or helping raise money for a charity.

Are there things about your character you would like to improve? For example, maybe you tend to be scared of trying new things. (Many of us are like that.) If you think you'd like to be more adventurous, pick something new and try it. Surround yourself with people who will support your efforts.

How Do I Set Goals for Myself?

We can all take little steps toward becoming the kind of person we want to be. The decisions you make now will powerfully shape the kind of adult you become. Don't underestimate your own capability to change and grow. Now that you are older, you can start setting goals for yourself. Setting goals is a great way to give yourself direction, accomplish a task or challenge, and make changes in your life.

Mentors and Role Models

Find as many positive role models and **mentors** as you can. A role model is someone you look up to and admire. A role model might be someone you know well, like a family member, a coach, or a member of your religious community. Because you admire that person, you use his or her life as inspiration for your own life. You can also have role models that you don't know personally, like celebrities. Role models can even be characters in books!

> " I really like that I am smart and a good writer. I am hoping to be a famous novelist someday. Right now I write poetry and short stories, and I am starting my first novel. I love to write and make people feel different things, and I like to make them laugh."
>
> Marie age 13

How to Set a Goal

- **Write down your goal.**
- **Set a timeline to accomplish your goal.** This might be up to you, or it might be set already. For example, if you are trying out for the soccer team, you already know the tryout date. If you want to get better at drawing, you'll have a less-defined timeline. Be realistic when thinking about how long accomplishing your goal will take.
- **Write down the steps you need to take to accomplish your goal.** If your goal is trying out for the soccer team, your steps might include an extra 30 minutes of practice every night, running three extra laps around the track every other day, and practicing ball handling on Saturday and Sunday.
- **Keep track of your progress.** Record the things you accomplish each day, week, or month as you head toward your goal.
- **Tell some trusted friends and adults about your goal and ask them for support.**
- **Even if you don't reach your goal, be sure to congratulate yourself for trying.** That's what matters most.

A mentor is someone who takes a more direct role in your life, giving you advice about how to take steps to get where you want to go. If you want to improve your singing, you might tell your music teacher, and she can become your mentor by giving you ideas and supporting your goal.

Dr. H says: "Role models and mentors help you feel empowered to create the best possible you. Positive mentors and role models are everywhere—just look around! Many people will be honored to help you become the person you want to be."

Quick Quiz
. . . .
When I establish a goal, I should only be happy with myself if I achieve that goal. True or False?

Going Through Puberty • A Girl's Manual for Body, Mind & Health

Enjoy the Ride

As you move through your teen years and beyond, listen to your inner judgment. You can be your own best friend when it comes to making good decisions and achieving your goals. Remember, you have family members and friends who will always be there for you as you grow and develop. Entering adulthood has its challenges, but it is also a great adventure as you learn, change, and grow. I wish you all the best as you enjoy the ride!

"Girls, you have your whole lives ahead of you. Remember, you have the power to shape yourself and your life any way you want. Be courageous and bold, and do all the things you can dream! Life is what you make it!"

—Lorna, mother of four

Just For Fun!

Start a Dreams and Goals Journal

Are there things you want to do and places you want to visit? Write them down. Start by brainstorming new activities you'd like to try. First, get out your journal and set a timer for 15 minutes. Then write down all the things you want to try but have never tried before, such as learning to make pottery, joining the swim team, taking a painting class, learning French, finding a pen pal in China, hiking up a mountain, meeting a new friend, running for class office, or trying out for the school play. Dream big, and then see if there's a way to make your dreams reality, step by step. Choose a goal, and then make a plan to accomplish it. Your goals can be little, like getting a good grade on your next science test, or big, such as becoming a nurse or doctor when you're older.

Resources

General Health

www.girlshealth.gov

Information on body, fitness, nutrition, feelings, bullying, relationships, and more. Created by the U.S. Department of Health and Human Services.

www.bam.gov

Information and games created by the Centers for Disease Control on diseases, physical activity, safety, making smart choices, and more.

www.kidshealth.org/

Designed for kids, teens, and parents— contains information on puberty, health, dealing with feelings, and more.

http://pbskids.org/itsmylife/

Includes videos, games, and information for kids on body, emotions, school, family, and friends.

Food, Exercise, and Drugs

Home Strength Training for Young Athletes (DVD-ROM) by Dr. Jordan Metzl. Resource for preteens and teens on beginning strength training produced by the American Academy of Pediatrics.

www.thecoolspot.gov

Provides information on alcohol and resisting peer pressure.

www.teens.drugabuse.gov

From the National Institute on Drug Abuse, provides facts on drugs and activities for teens.

Bullying, Stress, and Self-Esteem

www.stopbullying.gov

Interactive games to help kids understand and prevent bullying. Includes information for adults as well.

The Stress Reduction Workbook for Teens: Mindfulness Skills to Help You Deal with Stress by Gina Biegel (Instant Help, 2010). Contains activities that help young people reduce and manage their stress.

Glossary

A

Acne
A common skin condition that occurs when the pores of the skin become clogged with oil, dead skin cells, and bacteria; it typically includes blackheads, whiteheads, or pimples on the face, chest, or back.

Adipose tissue
A special group of cells commonly known as fat. These important cells store energy and protect and insulate other organs.

Adolescence
The period including and following the onset of puberty, during which a young person develops from a child into an adult. During adolescence your body, thoughts, feelings and behaviors will mature.

Areola
The dark colored part of the breast that surrounds the nipple.

Antiperspirant
A product to decrease body odor. It contains a substance (aluminum) that decreases the amount of sweat released onto the skin.

Anus
The opening where feces (poop) exit the body.

B

Benzoyl peroxide
An ingredient that works to kill the bacteria associated with acne formation.

Bullying
To use superior strength or influence to intimidate someone, typically to force him or her to do what you want.

C

Carbohydrates
Nutrients found in starchy foods, such as whole-grain breads, rice, bran muffins, potatoes, sweet potatoes, and pasta.

Cervix
Lower, narrow part of the uterus that connects the vagina to the rest of the uterus.

Character
The mental and moral qualities of your personality that define what kind of a person you are.

Clique (pronounced "click")
A small group of people with shared interests who spend time together and sometimes exclude others.

Clitoris
A female sexual organ. The clitoris is found where the labia minora (inner lips) meet.

Crush
Intense feelings of liking someone or being attracted to someone, usually not long lasting.

D

Deodorant
A product that has components that cover up body odor; may also contain ingredients that help inhibit the growth of bacteria, which decreases odor.

E

Eating disorders
Abnormal eating habits that might involve eating too much or too little and obsessing about food.

Estrogens
A special group of hormones especially important for female development and reproductive functions.

F

Fallopian (uterine) tubes
Arm-like structures that come out from both sides of the uterus and open to the inside of the body.

Fats
Nutrients found in butter, olive oil, canola oil, and margarine.

G

Growth spurt
A period of rapid growth.

H

Hair follicle
A "tunnel" lined with skin cells that usually contains a hair and opens to the skin.

Hormones
Signaling molecules made by your body that travel through the bloodstream to the cells of the body, helping control how the cells work.

Hymen
Thin layer covering most of the vaginal opening, found in most girls.

L

Labia
The inner and outer lips of the vagina. The labia cover and protect the other external reproductive organs.

Labia majora (outer lips)
The left and right thick outer folds of skin that cover and protect the other external reproductive organs.

Labia minora
Labia minora (inner lips)
The left and right thin inner folds of skin that cover and protect the other external reproductive organs.

M

Menarche
First time a girl menstruates or gets her period.

Menstruation (menses, menstrual cycle, period)
Time that occurs about once a month in women and girls, in which part of the lining of the uterus exits through the vagina; about one-quarter to one-third cup of blood is shed.

Mentor
A person who is an expert in an area that interests you and who takes on the active role of helping you reach your goals in this area.

Mood swings
Extreme or rapid changes in mood.

Mons (mons pubis)
The soft slightly raised area on the front of the pubic bone.

N

Nipple
A circular region about a centimeter across that sticks out a little from the rest of the breast.

Nutrients
Chemical substances found in food that your body needs to survive and thrive.

O

Ovaries
In a female, these are oval organs on both sides of the body attached to the uterus by a string-like tissue. They contain the ova.

Ovulation
In a mature woman, this is the process in which an ovum bursts out of the ovary about once a month.

Ovum
A single egg cell produced in a female's body. (**Ova** is the plural of ovum.)

P

Peer pressure
Pressure from one's peers (friends) to behave a certain way.

Premenstrual syndrome (PMS)
When a girl or woman has three or more negative symptoms in the week or two leading up to her period.

Pimple
Inflamed, raised region of the skin that's sore to the touch.

Proteins
Nutrients found in foods like meat; nuts; dairy products like milk, yogurt, and cheese; eggs; and beans.

Puberty
A normal phase of human development in which a child's body transitions into an adult's body.

Pubic hair
Hair that develops on and around the sex organs during puberty.

R

Razor bumps
Irritated, painful bumps that occur after shaving.

Razor burn
An irritating rash that appears a few minutes after shaving.

S

Salicylic acid
An acne treatment that helps prevent clogged hair follicles and unclog already-clogged follicles.

Sebaceous glands
Glands associated with hair follicles that make an oily product called sebum.

Sebum
An oily substance released by the sebaceous glands, which flows up from the hair follicle and out onto your skin or hair, creating increased oiliness.

Self-conscious
Excessively aware of being observed by others; feeling socially uncomfortable.

Self-esteem
Respect for oneself; having a favorable, positive view of oneself.

Sexual abuse
A type of illegal act when someone touches your private parts in an inappropriate way that makes you feel uncomfortable.

Stress
Physical or psychological tension.

U

Uterus
A hollow, triangle-shaped organ that connects the vagina and the fallopian tubes. This is where a baby develops during pregnancy.

V

Vagina
A muscular structure that connects the vaginal opening to the cervix.

Vaginal opening
An opening inside the inner lips, which opens into the vagina.

Vaginal discharge
A fluid from glands inside the vagina and cervix; it sweeps away bacteria and dead cells.

Vitamins and minerals
A group of nutrients found in fruits and vegetables and in some other foods.

Vulva
A female's external reproductive organs.

More Great Books from the
What Now? Series!

Lesson Ladder is dedicated to helping you prepare for life's most fundamental challenges. We provide practical tools and well-rounded advice that help achieve your goals while climbing the personal or professional ladder–whether it is preparing to start a family of your own or getting your child potty trained.

I'm Having a Baby! Well-Rounded Perspectives

Collective wisdom for a more comforting and "balanced" understanding of what to expect during pregnancy, childbirth, and the days that follow.
$19.99

I Had My Baby! A Pediatrician's Essential Guide to the First 6 Months

Gain confidence to experience the true joy of parenthood! From learning what to expect during those first minutes in the hospital through your baby's first 6 months, this concise, reader-friendly, and reassuring guide covers core topics you'll need to know as a new parent.
$16.99

Making Kid Time Count for Ages 0-3: The Attentive Parent Advantage

Whether you're a working or stay-at-home parent, this book shows you how to maximize your time with your baby or toddler with tips for developing a strong parent-child relationship, and ways to ensure strong cognitive, social, and emotional development for your child.
$16.99

I'm Potty Training My Child: Proven Methods That Work

Respecting that children and parenting styles differ, we created this guide to offer a variety of effective training solutions to help today's busy parents with easy, fast reading, and even faster results!
$12.99

Better Behavior for Ages 2-10: Small Miracles That Work Like Magic

For the harried parent, this book offers the compassion, help, and proven solutions you need to manage–and preven–difficult child behavior.
$16.99

Call toll-free to order! **1-800-301-4647**
Or order online: **www.LessonLadder.com**